THERAPY WITH

SETTING
BOUNDARIES

100 Ways to Protect Yourself, Strengthen Your Relationships, and Build the Life You Want…Starting Now!

KRYSTAL MAZZOLA WOOD, MEd, LMFT

Adams Media
New York   London   Toronto   Sydney   New Delhi

Adams Media
An Imprint of Simon & Schuster, Inc.
100 Technology Center Drive
Stoughton, Massachusetts 02072

First Adams Media trade paperback edition September 2023

ADAMS MEDIA and colophon are registered trademarks of Simon & Schuster, Inc.

For information about special discounts for bulk purchases, please contact Simon & Schuster Special Sales at 1-866-506-1949 or business@simonandschuster.com.

The Simon & Schuster Speakers Bureau can bring authors to your live event. For more information or to book an event, contact the Simon & Schuster Speakers Bureau at 1-866-248-3049 or visit our website at www.simonspeakers.com.

Interior design by Michelle Kelly
Images © 123RF

Manufactured in the United States of America

1 2023

Library of Congress Cataloging-in-Publication Data
Names: Mazzola, Krystal, author. | Adams Media (Firm), issuing body.
Title: Setting boundaries / Krystal Mazzola Wood, MEd, LMFT.
Description: Stoughton, Massachusetts: Adams Media, [2023] | Series: Therapy within reach | Includes bibliographical references and index.
Identifiers: LCCN 2023019625 | ISBN 9781507221334 (pb) | ISBN 9781507221327 (ebook)
Subjects: LCSH: Boundaries (Psychology) | Interpersonal relations--Psychological aspects. | Self-help techniques.
Classification: LCC BF697 .M399 2023 | DDC 155.2--dc23/eng/20230605
LC record available at https://lccn.loc.gov/2023019625

ISBN 978-1-5072-2133-4
ISBN 978-1-5072-2132-7 (ebook)

Dedication

To Amy—long before I ever believed I deserved self-protection, you never failed to affirm my right to it. You have been an integral part of my healing journey and my first experience of a healthy relationship. Our friendship is one of the greatest gifts of my life—thank you for being such a bright light—I love you.

Acknowledgments

Julia: Thank you so much for believing in my voice and vision in helping others establish healthy boundaries. I'm so grateful for your support and guidance as I developed and wrote this book. I sincerely appreciated the reliable container you provided me during the creative process. I hope that this is the first of many projects together.

Laura: You are an incredible editor. Thank you for understanding my vision completely. Your insights to clarify my words and intentions to support every reader are truly invaluable! I should be so lucky as to have your guidance in the future!

Caleb: You are the therapist who helped me course correct when I was on a path of self-sabotage. Thank you for your profound insights and support—you helped me change the entire trajectory of my life. Without you, I wouldn't be living into the authentic life of my dreams. Your work in this world is a precious gift—thank you for all you have done for me and, undoubtedly, countless other clients. You are appreciated.

Skitters: Thank you for your daily reminders of assertiveness in action.

Amy: Thank you for helping me find my voice. I love watching you deepen yours as well—it's so beautiful. Thank you for providing me moments of space from this project—I needed that!

My book club ladies: Jules, Tiffany, Carrie, Amra, Jasmine, Taylor, and Melanie—your friendships have deepened my confidence. Each of you is the embodiment of an authentic, trustworthy friend—thank you for always celebrating my voice with such genuine love and support.

All my clients past and present: This book wouldn't have been possible without you. Thank you for trusting me to walk beside you on your journey of healing and empowerment. Watching you find your authentic self and voice is awe-inspiring. You have enriched my life more than you know.

Ethan: When we first started dating, I was so amazed—and still am—by your commitment to your self-protection. You always inspire me in the way you never doubt your right to your boundaries. Thank you for being such a consistent role model of empowerment. There are no words for my gratitude for your support during my book-writing process (now I've written more with you than without you!). Thank you for believing in me and my vision to have a positive ripple effect in this world. Your friendship and partnership is truly what I always dreamed of. I love you!

Contents

Introduction

Do you find yourself saying yes to too many requests? Frustrated by a meddling in-law or parent? Overtired, undernourished, or stressed? You may need to learn to set better boundaries. Setting healthy boundaries allows you to establish limits on the influence others have on your life and to make choices about what's right for you. Boundaries can look like saying no to an invitation, standing up for yourself with loved ones, asserting your needs in a relationship, and taking care of your body. *Therapy Within Reach: Setting Boundaries* will teach you why you need boundaries in every area of your life—from your relationships to your health to your work—and how to set them.

Taking the steps to have healthier boundaries is courageous. You may feel a little intimidated or uncertain as you begin this journey, but *Therapy Within Reach: Setting Boundaries* makes the process easy to understand and can support you whether you work alongside a therapist or alone. If your budget or schedule makes therapy difficult to incorporate into your life, allow this book to be your step-by-step guide as you transform your life.

Throughout this book, much like in therapy, you will gain greater self-awareness. This self-awareness empowers you to acquire many necessary skills for boundary setting. For example, when you know yourself better, the boundaries you need are easier to identify. The self-confidence that comes with self-awareness allows you to communicate your limits effectively with others in a kind, clear, and loving way. Self-awareness also empowers you to overcome personal barriers to setting limits, including guilt and anxiety. You'll learn that setting boundaries is not selfish or unfriendly—in fact, it's the best way to build relationships based in honesty. Finally, the more you know about yourself, the more you care about yourself. Greater self-love assists you in setting boundaries as you become increasingly committed to self-protection.

Boundary setting is a skill that requires taking action, so you will find one hundred hands-on activities in this book. These exercises provide concrete opportunities to develop and practice your boundary-setting skills in quick and simple ways. For example, you'll learn how to:

- Overcome any guilt that's preventing you from setting boundaries
- Discover which specific boundaries you need and why
- Say no without being hostile
- Clearly and confidently communicate your limits to others
- Push back when your boundaries are not respected
- And more

Therapy Within Reach: Setting Boundaries will teach you how to identify what you need and don't need in your life. Just like you can develop and strengthen muscles, you will develop and strengthen your ability to set boundaries in a way that feels natural and intuitive. These skills will serve you well throughout your life, as the need to set, express, and adjust boundaries never goes away. Your ongoing commitment to boundaries will help you build healthy relationships, boost your confidence, and create a happy and well-balanced life.

How to Use This Book

Going to therapy is a powerful and courageous way to learn more about yourself, prioritize your mental health, and overcome life's challenges. The Therapy Within Reach series allows you to explore important mental health topics in the comfort of your own home, at your own pace. Whether you are considering going to therapy or are years into your practice, the hands-on, practical exercises in *Therapy Within Reach: Setting Boundaries* can help you reinforce key ideas, practice new skills, and accelerate your progress.

While it's not necessary to attend therapy while using this book, a professional therapist can help you face particularly difficult challenges along the way. After all, a therapist who knows you and your situation is best qualified to assess and address your individual needs.

Therapy Within Reach: Setting Boundaries is set up in an easy-to-follow way. Chapters 1 and 2 provide the background information you'll need for the rest of this book, including what boundaries look like, the reasons they're necessary, and how to stay committed to them—even when it's challenging. You are then free to explore the rest of the chapters in any way that works for you. You can proceed through the book chapter by chapter or jump directly to topics and activities that resonate with you. There is no wrong choice.

During the process of learning to set boundaries, you may uncover some difficult aspects of your life that you have not fully processed yet. Be patient and kind with yourself. It's important to listen to—and honor—your thoughts and emotions. Reflect on these ideas fully and honestly and ask for help if you need it.

Whether you are using this book with a therapist or alone, it can open your eyes to new insights and ideas that can improve your physical and mental well-being. You are tremendously brave to choose to cultivate better boundaries. This is challenging but rewarding work that is worth your effort. Let *Therapy Within Reach: Setting Boundaries* be your gentle guide on this important journey.

PART 1

Getting Started

When you're just starting out on any journey, it's wise to prepare yourself. In Part 1, you will cultivate essential knowledge and skills to serve your entire boundary-setting journey throughout this book and beyond. It's natural to have more questions than answers right now, not only about how to set boundaries but what you authentically want. You will learn a lot about yourself throughout this process: You will connect fully with your goals and develop skills to keep you motivated even when you feel uncomfortable or challenged on the road ahead. You will learn how to encourage yourself while keeping yourself accountable to doing what's healthy for you.

This part will also encourage you to envision the future of your dreams. You may not even know what that looks like yet, which is understandable. Maybe you've been told before you're not being realistic when you've dreamed aloud—this book will help you ignore the naysayers and achieve the authentic life of your dreams. Please know that just by being here, you've already started changing your life with your courage to try to improve your boundary-setting skills.

CHAPTER 1

Laying the Foundation for Healthy Boundaries

Boundaries impact every aspect of your life and allow you to feel safe, relaxed, and loved. But there is more to boundaries than that—there are external and internal boundaries, and it's important to know how to make them "just right"...in other words, not too shaky or too strong.

In this chapter, you will learn all of the fundamentals of a healthy boundary system so you can build your knowledge base and confidence. These essential concepts will set you up for success as you address the more specific topics (such as boundaries around time, money, and so on) in the rest of the book.

What Are Boundaries?

In self-care terms, boundaries are any limit you need to set to feel safe. They are related to your unique needs, wants, and values. Boundaries are also connected to your authenticity. Living as you truly want to requires you to make choices about what works for you and what doesn't. Sometimes, your limits become clear from your gut or heart rather than being a conscious choice.

Boundaries—when healthy—are always present. They also exist in every relationship you have, including the one you have with yourself. Healthy boundaries are consistent, yet flexible. They may differ depending on the relationship, your mood, time of day, and your negotiable needs and wants. You may be extroverted, for example, yet still need your space at times.

Boundaries are like a fence around your house that allows you to feel protected from others. You decide who comes in and who stays out. But healthy boundaries are a fence—not a wall. You should be firm with your limits, but when it feels right, you may compromise too. For example, your doctor's office may have a policy of charging you for late cancellations. They may enforce this regularly, which is a solid boundary. Yet if there is an urgent need for you to cancel, your doctor may waive the fee. This is your doctor's healthy boundaries in action, as they are consistent yet flexible.

Boundaries work involves the rights you have alongside the responsibilities you have to others. You have the right to your needs and limits, *and* you have the responsibility to communicate these kindly. Rather than criticizing your spouse for being "lazy," for example, you may ask them to clean up after themselves. The basis of all healthy relationships is a sense of mutual safety.

Finally, a healthy boundaries system is comprised of two parts: external and internal limits. Let's learn more about each.

Understanding External Boundaries

External boundaries protect you from other people and act like the fence around your house, keeping you safe. They may be expressed directly at times—for example, if you ask a friend to let you know when they are running late in the future, this is an expressed external boundary.

Other times, however, you may choose not to express an external boundary that you still enforce, for a variety of reasons such as:

- Sometimes it just won't be an option to do so. If someone cuts you off in traffic, you won't be able to tell them assertively you need your safety respected. Yet at the same time, you may choose to switch lanes and avoid that car as best as possible in order to feel your safety is being respected.
- Sometimes it isn't necessary to express your external limit. Your own validation of your boundary—in other words, supporting its legitimacy—is enough to make you feel secure. For example, if you are avoiding diet culture, you may distance yourself in a conversation if someone is labeling foods as good or bad. You may choose

not to assert your limit because you don't need the other person to stop. Your own understanding—and respect—of your limit may be enough for you to take steps to feel safe.

- Finally, there are some situations or people with whom it's not safe to set limits directly. If you know certain people will argue with you or degrade you for setting boundaries, it's best to avoid expressing them directly to this person. You have a right to your boundaries and to feel safe. Part of this right to safety is discerning who is safe to set limits with and who is not. Let's say you have a coworker who bullies others. You may choose to avoid them rather than directly telling them you prefer kind communication. The way others—or you—respond to a boundary being set or a need being expressed is what separates safe people from unsafe people. In Chapter 9, you will learn more about how to discern safe people from unsafe ones.

Understanding Internal Boundaries

Internal limits are the boundaries you set on yourself to be safe. There are two parts to this:

1 The limits you set to be safe for others—for example, you may avoid saying things out of anger.
2 The limits you set to be safe for you—for example, you may practice self-care and self-soothing, perhaps by taking a walk to clear your head.

The basis of all healthy relationships is a sense of mutual safety, and internal boundaries help you maintain that.

Two Common Types of Boundary Problems

Here are two problems that many people experience with boundaries:

1 **Porous boundaries** are those that may exist in some situations, or times, but not others. A porous boundary might look like telling people personal, vulnerable information about yourself you wouldn't want shared too early in a relationship. People-pleasing

is also a sign of a porous boundary because in the name of making others happy, you might forget to give yourself this same care.

2 **Walled-off boundaries** look like an inability to be vulnerable or trust others despite signs they are trustworthy.

You may experience both of these situations with different boundaries: In some situations you may be walled off, and in others, too porous. You may also have healthy boundaries in some relationships or environments, or you might have violated someone else's boundary. No person follows a clear, linear path with their boundary concerns. This imperfection is human. Please try to avoid criticizing or attacking yourself. The most important thing is you are building greater awareness now to be safer moving forward. Finally, know that there are no "right" or "wrong" boundaries, as these are connected to your own personal preferences.

Learning how to set boundaries is about progress, never perfection (which is not possible for us humans!). Learning to develop greater understanding of healthy boundaries, and deeper self-awareness, are important wins in this journey.

Visualize Your Boundaries

In this exercise, you will visualize your boundaries as a bubble that is solid yet flexible. This enables you to think about boundaries as firm and consistent parameters to feel safe, while also being open to negotiating with others whenever possible to meet both of your needs. Once you have read through this visualization, try repeating it daily—especially when you are interacting with difficult people or in situations that overwhelm you. This visualization will help you feel more grounded and secure as you face those challenges.

Tools:
Piece of paper and a writing utensil (optional)

Steps:

1 Find a comfortable seat and put both feet on the ground to enable you to feel more emotionally grounded. You may do this however you feel most comfortable—whether that's inside, with bare feet, with shoes on, or on the earth. If you have a hard time with visualizations, please put both feet on the ground and instead of using your imagination, write out the next prompts in the first person, adding in the details you want.

2 Imagine a marker in any color you prefer in your hand. Picture yourself drawing a circle all the way around yourself on the ground. Take a deep breath. If you are writing this out, you may write *I'm sitting down with a red marker. Now I'm drawing a red circle on the ground around me.* (Please continue in that manner for the rest of the exercise.)

3 Imagine the circle turns into light and begins to rise up all the way around you. This light may be the same color as your marker or a different one. Whatever you see, please know this is right. See this light continuing to grow all the way around you until it is up to your knees and the back of your seat.

4 As you inhale, allow this light to grow up over your chest and the base of your throat and neck.

5 Imagine this circle growing over your face and the back of your head. This light continues to grow until it connects over the crown of your head, forming a bubble. It should connect all the way around you. If there are any gaps in your bubble, please visualize patching it with what feels right—perhaps with flowers or a piece of satin.

6 While in your bubble, you decide what you allow into your life and your emotional experience. You are protected from others' judgments, expectations, problems, and desires. You choose what works for you and what does not. You also have a filter in this bubble that enables you to respect others' boundaries. Finally, inside this bubble, you are free to authentically update your limits or negotiate whenever this feels right.

7 Notice how you feel emotionally in your bubble. What sensations are you aware of in your body? Hopefully, you feel safe and comfortable. If not, please imagine what you may bring into your bubble to feel safer. This should not be another person in your life, though, as this prevents healthy intimacy. This is because genuine intimacy requires each person to have their own separate space. It's only with this separate space that you can hear and see the other person clearly. Otherwise, they are too close to be truly seen. Rather, you could call in a pet, your higher power, or your future self to comfort you. Explore what allows you to feel safest inside your bubble.

8 Even as you end the visualization, you can always imagine having this bubble in place. Whenever you feel overwhelmed, check in to see if your protective bubble is up. If not, redo this visualization to re-create it.

Reconnect with Your Body

When you have porous boundaries, your thoughts may center on taking care of others or gaining their approval. This external focus may lead you to feel disconnected from yourself, both emotionally and physically. Sadly, this hinders your ability to identify your boundaries, as these limits can only come from you. In this activity, you will practice reconnecting with your body in the present moment so you can refocus your attention on your needs.

Steps:

1 Take a moment to center yourself in a way that works for you. This can mean taking a couple deep breaths, putting your feet on the ground, or placing your hands on your heart to focus you on the current moment. Ask yourself, *Out of 100 percent of me, how much is present right now?* You will likely see, hear, or just know this number. Most people, especially those with porous boundaries, are not 100 percent present. There is no shame in this.

2 As you breathe in, notice where you feel your consciousness is residing (most people choose their head). Now imagine pulling your attention down from your head and shoulders into the soles of your feet and toes.

3 Spread your presence into your arms, hands, and fingertips.

4 Now pull your attention inward and notice any sensations (such as tingles) that may or may not be present in your feet and hands.

5 Feel yourself fully inhabiting your body. Squeeze your fingers and toes and then gently release to notice your presence in your body.

6 Take a deep breath to notice the difference physically, and potentially emotionally, when you bring your consciousness more fully into your body. Notice whatever is your truth right now, even if that sensation is discomfort. Simply notice this as information while celebrating yourself for deepening your connection to your body.

Imagine You're a Child and Protect Yourself

Setting boundaries effectively is almost like parenting yourself. A healthy parent only allows trusted people to watch their child. And if/when their child says they hurt, they attentively listen and take action to protect their child. If you had parents who guided and protected you, then you can use their actions as a model. If not, please know you are not alone—and you are completely capable of becoming a healthy parent toward yourself. In this exercise, you'll act like a parent to empower yourself to provide the protection you need and deserve.

Tools:
Piece of paper and a writing utensil

Steps:

1 What situations would you remove yourself from if you were acting as a healthy parent toward yourself? This could be an overly demanding job, for example. You don't need to justify why these situations aren't good for you. If these situations hurt "the child," this is enough to warrant boundaries.

2 Are there any people you would limit your "child's" time around? Examples of this could be a toxic friend or a bullying coworker.

3 Your responses reveal the limits you may need to set. If you're not ready to do that yet, it's all right. Simply building your awareness over what hurts is a critical step toward boundary setting.

4 Now, turn your attention to your inner child. This is the playful, childlike part of you. Building this connection may feel strange, silly, or awkward, but opening up lines of communication with this part of yourself helps deepen your willingness to self-protect. Imagine validating, or supporting, this child by writing them a kind note. Let them know you completely understand why this person, or people, overwhelms them. Validate that there is nothing wrong with being overwhelmed by certain people or situations. Tell this child they have a right to their feelings.

5 To end the note, comfort the child by letting them know you are learning skills to give them the protection they deserve.

Set Internal Limits to Be Safe with Yourself

The internal limits we'll explore in this exercise are those boundaries you set to be safe for yourself, such as self-care. Many people overlook these or see them as selfish, when in fact they are the exact opposite. In this activity, you will reflect on areas where you might be able to improve your internal limits.

Tools:
Piece of paper and a writing utensil

Steps:

1 Divide your piece of paper into three horizontal sections labeled Areas for Growth, Reasons, and Goals. Under Areas for Growth, list areas in your life where you feel like you aren't showing up for yourself the way you'd like. For example, you may not be getting enough sleep, or maybe you haven't scheduled an important doctor's appointment. Try to notice this with accepting curiosity and just focus on becoming aware of these situations.

2 Provide yourself understanding about the reasons you may sometimes overlook yourself, listing these in the second section of the paper. Being overworked, lacking financial resources, or being overwhelmed are all understandable reasons you may forget to take care of yourself.

3 In the Goals area of your paper, brainstorm one way you'd like to show up for yourself more, and a baby step you can take toward this goal. For example, if you want to exercise more, you may commit to walking twice a week, which is tremendous progress!

Set Internal Limits to Be Safe with Others

Setting internal limits to be safe with others refers to how you will behave in order to make other people feel safe around you. For example, you may want to avoid saying things when you're angry. We're all human, so we will all make mistakes and violate others' boundaries sometimes. But if you have porous boundaries, you are much more likely to be overwhelmed by those mistakes—even if they are unintentional—than to recognize the truth that others will do the same to you. In this activity, you will follow a six-step framework for being safe for others as best as possible by minimizing shame.

Steps:

1 **Remember a time you violated a boundary.** To begin this exercise, recall a time when you violated someone else's boundaries, even if accidentally. If you can't think of anything, ask yourself, *Has anyone in my life recently told me that I hurt, upset, or offended them?* Maybe your daughter has asked you to stop forcing her to play soccer. Perhaps your spouse has let you know that they feel you don't listen to them.

2 **Notice your feelings.** Now carefully observe how this situation makes you feel. Many people feel ashamed. This is different from guilt, which is the feeling of "I did a bad thing." Shame, on the other hand, makes you believe you are a "bad person."

3 **Observe how you treat yourself.** Think about how you are treating yourself as a result of this situation. Some people are very hard on themselves when they feel ashamed, guilty, or embarrassed. Remember, the very nature of being human is to be imperfect. You will naturally make mistakes, including violating others' limits at times, simply because you are human.

4 **Practice self-compassion.** Practice saying no to the critical voice that may be telling you how "bad" you are right now. This type of shame attack prevents you from being safe for yourself. It also prevents you from giving those around you the very safety you want to give them. When you don't set limits around that critical voice, it's natural to want to defend your actions to "prove" you're good rather than validating where you may have been hurtful to someone.

5 Identify any defensiveness. Notice if you have the urge to defend or justify your actions that have upset others. Defensiveness invalidates the other person's feelings and boundaries, leaving them more upset. Try to assess the situation like a robot trying to gather the facts.

6 Be accountable. All people violate others' boundaries at times, but what separates safe people from unsafe ones is the ability to take genuine accountability. In your situation, what can you take accountability for without falsely apologizing or being defensive? Genuine accountability includes an apology alongside steps to change. What can you do to be a safe person for the people in your life you may have hurt? For example:

- You could apologize to your daughter and validate that she has the right to choose the after-school activities that bring her joy. As her parent, you still have the responsibility to guide her, so you may also validate the importance of movement and encourage her to identify what other exercise she likes.
- You could tell your spouse that you hear what they're saying and admit that you've been distracted. You may let them know you value connection too and will dedicate twenty minutes a night to just being with them—without screens.

Learn Different Communication Methods

There are four primary ways of communicating: passive, passive-aggressive, aggressive, and assertive communication. Ultimately, all but assertive communication are unsafe forms of communicating with others. They are unsafe for you because you don't get your needs met and they're unsafe for others because they're not respectful. These ineffective forms of communicating lead to misunderstandings, preventable conflict, and resentment—and they're a common reason couples seek out therapy.

In this activity, you will explore your personal habits of communicating to gain awareness and increase your sense of safety while respecting others. Remember, everyone is imperfect, and everyone makes mistakes. No matter how much you have practiced effective boundary-setting skills, you will communicate ineffectively at times. This is a process of progress, not perfection.

Tools:

TV show or movie

Piece of paper and a writing utensil, or a digital notepad

Steps:

1 Take some time to watch a TV show or movie. This can be the next episode in a series you're watching, an old favorite, or something unfamiliar. When you watch this show, you will act as a detective, noting what types of communication are being used at any given time. You may feel uncertain at times and that's completely okay. Simply note which one of the four main styles of communicating you hear when they're clear. Try to find at least one example of each. Write down what you heard that highlighted the specific type of communication (e.g., "The guy she was dating said 'If you don't do this for me, you don't love me,' and that's aggressive."). Here are the four styles:

- **Passive communication** is when you don't speak up for what you need, want, or feel. Here you are silent and don't express your needs or limits at all. You may notice that this type of communicating happens more frequently in certain situations or with certain people. You may notice more what someone *isn't* saying more than what they *are* saying when you hear passive communication in others.

- **Passive-aggressive communication** is when you don't clearly express your needs—you may guilt others, make "jokes," or slip in subtle comments, hoping others will pick up on your needs or limits. You may hear others gossiping, being sarcastic, or mocking someone when they are being passive-aggressive. Or they might use body language such as rolling their eyes.
- **Aggressive communication** includes yelling, criticizing others, or making threats. A person may act like a bully or cutthroat when they are being aggressive. Remember, all people are imperfect, so try to withhold judgment. A person's body language may look intimidating such as glaring, pointing fingers, or clenching their fists or jaw when they're being aggressive.
- When you use **assertive communication**, you directly tell people what you need, want, expect, or what your boundaries are in a way that's safe for you and them. Assertive communication allows people to clearly hear your needs while minimizing their potential urge to be defensive because they feel respected. When you hear this in others, they are clear, kind, direct, and honest about their thoughts, feelings, needs, and wants with the listener. They also are respectful of the listener's viewpoints.

2 Once you have at least one example for each type of communication, ask yourself some questions:
- How did you feel watching the non-assertive communication styles in others? Did any make you feel overwhelmed or cringe? Notice how it's understandable that others, and you, could sometimes speak in ways that aren't assertive for various reasons. Also notice how non-assertive communication may overwhelm, upset, confuse, or anger the listener, leading to less effective interactions.
- What was the impact you observed of assertive communication on relationships compared to non-assertive communication?
- When you heard assertive communication, how did this feel? Notice that even if you're not in the practice of being consistently assertive yet, it's completely possible to learn. As you move forward in this book, you will find many opportunities to communicate more effectively by using assertive communication. Practice being courageous and open-minded when these opportunities arise.

Assert Your Limits

Assertive communication is when you clearly and kindly express your needs and limits instead of hiding or minimizing your needs and potentially resenting others for not reading your mind. Once you've made the courageous decision to speak up kindly, the next steps are straightforward. The intention of this exercise is to show the clear, simple script for assertive communication. However, please know, at this stage of your journey, there's no need to practice this yet, unless you feel ready. Right now, as is common with therapy skills and concepts, you are simply planting seeds to know how to assert yourself when you choose. Feel free to come back to this exercise when you have more practice setting limits internally.

In this activity, you will learn a simple script to assert your limits. You will also plan for common potential outcomes.

Steps:

1 Identify your boundary. Anger (including frustration, annoyance, or resentment) is your clearest sign of a boundary you need to set.

2 Prepare yourself for the conversation. Above all, plan to keep it simple. If you say too much, you risk diluting your message and backing down. You also don't want to give in to the urge to make excuses, justify, or defend your boundary. Otherwise, you increase the chances of overwhelming, confusing, or making the listener defensive.

3 You may modify the following script as needed to assert yourself but please keep it short. Boundaries are meaningless without consequences. However, you might only be ready to state the positive outcome of being respected for now. Decide what makes sense for you. But keep the negative consequences in mind. Unless you are willing to set consequences for violating your boundaries, asserting yourself is meaningless. People learn how they can treat you by what you allow.

   - State the situation objectively, and you may validate the other person briefly as appropriate. You may also quickly share your feelings.
   - Then state, "I need (or want) [your boundary]. I'm hoping this is respected. If so, [state the positive consequence of respecting your limit]. If not, [mention the negative consequence of disrespecting your boundary]." Here's an example:

- I feel annoyed that my brother's been really pushy about his opinions lately as to what I should do in my marriage. I need him to accept that I have the right to make my own choices and don't want to discuss this anymore. I will assert this to him with this script:
- "I know I told you I've been having issues with my husband. I completely understand why you've been giving me advice since then on what I should do, but lately it's been overwhelming me. I need to figure out my own path. I hope you can stop giving me advice right now so that I can feel less stressed when we talk. Otherwise, I will need to end our calls if you start giving me advice about my marriage.

4 If your limit is respected, great!

5 If not (intent does not matter), consider the frequency of the violation:
- Rare violations: Please know that even safe people make mistakes. Are they truly making steps to change but slipped up? If so, remind this person of your boundary.
- Consistent disregard of your limit: If your boundary is consistently disregarded, this is when to implement the consequence. For example, ending the phone call. When you set a boundary, you will discover how safe or unsafe a person or environment is for you. For extra support if your boundaries are disrespected, please see Chapter 9.

Create Your Boundaries Treasure Map

In many movies and books, a treasure map shows the hero or heroine how to find their reward, such as jewels or gold. In your journey, you are pursuing something even more valuable—peace, authenticity, and well-being. You are accomplishing all this—and more—by learning how to set boundaries effectively and consistently.

In this exercise, you will create your treasure map, which will provide a clear pathway for your personal transformation process. All you need to do is keep referencing your treasure map to guide you as you develop boundary-setting skills. You could also consider it your treatment plan. (In therapy, it is standard practice to create a treatment plan where you outline your goals and how you will accomplish them.)

Tools:
Markers, crayons, or colored pencils
Piece of unlined paper or construction paper

Steps:

1 Take a moment to consider your primary reason(s) for picking up this book. What are the concerns you want to address? Write down these concerns somewhere on the left side of the paper. If you have many concerns, write down the top three.

2 When these concerns are resolved, what will be different in your life? (Doing the Write the Story of Your Future Self exercise in Chapter 2 might help you generate some ideas.) Write down your ultimate goal on the right side of your paper and mark this spot with an X.

3 How will you be able to tell that you've made progress toward your goal? Consider the smaller signs that will show that you are on the road to healing. Draw a meandering line from your concerns on the left side of the page to your goal on the right side. Write down these smaller signs of progress at various points along this pathway.

4 Now review this book's table of contents. While all the chapters are valuable, listen to yourself to identify which chapters are most needed to accomplish your goals. Allow yourself to trust your *feelings* of what to read to meet each smaller sign of progress. Note these chapters near each goal.

5 Keep your treasure map handy moving forward, such as on your nightstand. Trust you have created the right path for you and follow the steps you outlined. Keep this treasure map until the end of this book— you'll review it later.

Example of key points on a map:

Left side of paper: I want to stop people-pleasing.
Right side of paper with X marking the spot: I will take time for self-care. I can say no without guilt. I can tell my spouse or parents my needs.
Along the line drawn: I am making progress when I…
- Can tell my parents I can't visit this summer (Chapters 8, 9, and 10)
- Start reading again for pleasure (Chapters 4, 5, and 6)
- Let my husband know I need more help at home (Chapters 8, 9, and 10)

Change Takes Time

The change process is typically not linear. You might feel discouraged when you experience natural setbacks or see few results despite hard work at first. Please be patient with yourself and stay committed—the change process is initially slow, but then gains momentum.

CHAPTER 2

Staying Focused

Before you begin work on boundaries themselves, it's a good idea to prepare yourself for this task. The activities in this chapter will help you focus your energy, clear away some potential roadblocks, and stay motivated and committed even when the road ahead is strenuous. You'll learn how to envision your success, be your own cheerleader, and get rid of old habits or patterns that aren't serving you well now.

If you ever find your sense of commitment to setting boundaries faltering, come back to this chapter and its activities. You can remind yourself exactly why you began this journey of empowerment, reconnect with your hopeful vision for the future, and recharge your motivation. The activities in this chapter will encourage and support you.

The power to change your life exists within you. The first steps begin now.

What Can Boundaries Do for You?

Developing healthy boundaries can profoundly transform your life. For example:

- When you set boundaries, you begin to have time and space to live as your authentic self. This space and self-awareness allows you to effectively change anything in your life that no longer works for you.
- Healthy boundaries teach you that you are the best—and only—person capable of directing your life in a way that is authentically fulfilling.

- Boundaries can help you and the people you interact with feel heard and respected.
- By learning how to prioritize self-care—an important part of setting boundaries—you'll actually experience greater emotional stability and improved physical health.

As you start this journey, the most important thing to remember is that you have the right to protect yourself with boundaries. You have the right to heal your life and improve any relationships or situations that cause you pain. You have the right—even the responsibility—to make the changes necessary that you need to find peace even without others' approval or change.

If you don't set boundaries, you might find that you feel anxious, tired, or overwhelmed; powerless and stuck; or unsure and prone to second-guessing yourself. In a bigger-picture sense, you might find it difficult to find true happiness or you might feel like someone or something is missing from your life. When you avoid setting the boundaries you need, the likely outcome is only greater anxiety, insecurity, and/or resentment. You may find yourself acting in ways that don't seem like who you really are. Commonly, this may manifest as finding yourself hiding or ignoring your feelings because you want to "pick your battles" or not upset others. Yet later you find yourself exploding at the other person. Maybe you yell or you launch into a laundry list of all the things you're upset about with them—not just the issue at hand. Or you may be passive-aggressive, making "jokes" or being sarcastic at others' expense, hoping they will figure out what you need. Alternatively, you may never let your resentment come out and instead, you may always hide your true thoughts and feelings to the point of total self-disconnection and even depression. None of these options are good for your physical or mental health—that's why boundary setting is so important.

Finding Solutions to Common Roadblocks

If you struggle to not only set boundaries but even to know how to identify your limits, this is completely understandable. You are not alone, either. Many people reach adulthood without learning these skills. Don't worry; this book will help you develop greater insight into your needs and boundaries. Here are some common challenges people face as they think about setting boundaries:

Roadblock: You worry that setting boundaries is "mean" or that they'll ruin your relationships.

Solution: Understand that this couldn't be further from the truth. In fact, it's when you *don't* set boundaries that your relationships suffer. Boundaries can help both parties feel heard and respected. Boundary setting is an act of love, both for yourself and anyone you're in a relationship with, romantic or otherwise. Your sense of intimacy with others deepens as each of you reveal more of who you truly are by sharing your needs and limits honestly.

Roadblock: You feel guilty putting your own needs first.

Solution: Learning how to prioritize self-care will help you stabilize your emotions and improve your physical health. Your increased well-being also naturally benefits the people you love as you can be more present in their lives for longer.

Roadblock: You struggle with conflicting feelings.

Solution: Accept that it's completely natural to have a part of you that also feels unkind for developing your limits, even if you know you need them. Having two feelings at once—also known as dialectical thinking—is completely possible. Dialectical thinking reveals that one or more things that seem like opposites can both be true at the same time. You can love your spouse *and* resent them, for example. You may feel guilty setting boundaries *and* be improving your relationships by doing so. This type of thinking is an important tool to lean on as you cultivate your boundaries.

All of these challenges are common—and you can overcome them all. Boosting your confidence, focusing on self-care, and visualizing your happy future can help you work through difficult times.

Staying the Course

The activities in this chapter are designed to reinforce your commitment to developing boundaries whenever you feel challenged. At times, you may experience natural confusion or doubt over your limits. Other times, the people in your life may challenge or disrespect your limits. When these issues arise, come back to these activities to remind you why this process matters to have the life you truly want.

When you are truly healing, you might first feel like your life is becoming *worse* rather than better. This is a natural stage during the change process. It's precisely when you feel more uncomfortable emotions, believe some relationships are worsening, or find your fuse is shorter than ever that you are actually truly becoming empowered.

You have so much to look forward to on this journey. A life with more autonomy and happiness is ahead of you! The skills you develop in this chapter keep you committed to ensure you reap all the benefits of your hard work.

Write the Story of Your Future Self

Whenever you work toward improving yourself, it's important to have your destination in mind. Just as you don't get in your car without an end goal, the same is true for a successful boundary-setting journey. Of course, you also want to keep an open mind during this process, but having clear intentions will make your path clearer.

In this activity, you will envision your future self, who is skilled at boundary setting. Rereading this vision later will help keep you motivated through the natural ups and downs of the process.

Tools:
Piece of paper and a writing utensil
Digital vision board such as *Pinterest* (optional)

Steps:

1 For this exercise, you'll take about twenty minutes to imagine and write down the details of where you would like this journey to take you by envisioning a day in your future. (If you are a visual person, you can answer these questions by assembling images in an online program or app.) Allow yourself to simply feel curious. You need not worry about *how* you will accomplish what you see. As you imagine your future reality, please know there doesn't need to be anything wrong with your current one. You may feel grateful for the life you already have, *and* some changes may be useful for your growth.

2 These prompts might help you spark ideas:
   • Contemplate a day in your future where you have healthy boundaries. Consider how, and when, you awaken. Do you have any morning rituals to care for yourself? If so, what are these practices? How do they help you?
   • On this future day, who do you spend time with? How has this relationship changed if you currently know this person? If it's a new person, imagine the quality of this relationship. See if any other details about your relationships in general arise.
   • How do you communicate with others now that you have healthy boundaries? Is it possible to be strong and kind?

- What is your relationship with yourself now like? How do you care for your mental and physical health? Consider how you will feel both physically and emotionally when you have healthy boundaries.
- In this future reality, what do you do for fun? Perhaps it's an activity you already enjoy but you may be devoting more time or space to it.
- On this future day with healthy boundaries, what do you do for work? This may be paid or unpaid contributions to your family and community. Are you connected to a sense of purpose? What do you need to feel respected, valued, and safe in your work?
- Finally, how do you end this day when you have healthy boundaries? Do you have any rituals to relax you? If so, what are they? How do they help you?

3 In your journal or on the piece of paper, write out all the details of what you envision. Reread this account of your future reality whenever you need a reminder as to why you are doing this work.

Set Small Goals

What is one small change that would move you closer to your vision? If you envisioned that you would have more energy in your future, for example, you might have imagined yourself going to bed an hour earlier. Perhaps you could initiate this change by going to bed ten minutes earlier today. Remember, all successful journeys begin with a single small step.

Build Hope with an Anchor Word

When you begin transformation work, it's natural to have more than one feeling at once. For example, one part of you may feel hopeful, while another part may feel uncertain if it's even possible for you to develop healthy boundaries. This mindset is completely understandable. To stay committed to your growth, you just need your hopeful part to be at least 1 percent bigger than your skeptical part.

To support your success, you will nurture your hopeful part in this activity by designating an "anchor word." An anchor word can help keep you grounded, focused, and hopeful about the task ahead. If you ever question your commitment, come back to your anchor word. It will center and calm you in the midst of a choppy sea.

Tools:

Writing utensil

Sticky note

Steps:

1 Consider your future reality, where you can set boundaries well. What word best represents how you will feel? Examples include: peaceful, confident, strong, relieved, light, energized, and calm. Pick a word that *feels* right—learning to trust yourself is a boundary-setting skill. You cannot pick a "wrong" word.

2 Write this word on a sticky note. Keep this note in a place you will often see it.

3 If you feel inspired, you may take your anchor word one step further. Identify an object that represents your anchor word—for example, a candle might represent *peaceful* or a particular accessory might make you feel *confident*. Imagine breathing the energy of your anchor word into this object. Use this item whenever you want support on your boundary-setting journey.

Find Your Boundary-Setting Role Model

When you are developing a new skill, it's helpful to look at others who have established expertise in this area. Just as you may watch clips of Serena Williams if you want to master tennis, you can learn from someone who sets boundaries in a way that you admire.

Tools:
Photo of or object related to your role model

Steps:

1 Consider who may be your boundaries role model. This may be a person whose self-assuredness you admire. This person likely is not bound by other people's judgments or expectations. They also may balance their love for others with self-love. It could be a person you already know, such as a friend, a family member, a therapist, a teacher, a coach. If you cannot identify anyone in your life, consider TV or movie characters who are assertive yet kind. Keep in mind that you cannot pick an incorrect role model.

2 Find a photo of the person or identify an object that you associate with this person. For example, you might wear an article of clothing similar to something a TV character wears. Use this physical reminder of your role model when you want to connect with their qualities during a challenging moment.

3 Moving forward, think about this person or character when you need to set a boundary. Consider how this person might think and act. What qualities would they embody as they set this boundary? Imagine that you could speak to them about a concern you have. How would they respond? What encouragement or guidance would they provide?

4 Your role model may evolve over time as your skills develop. Don't hesitate to revisit this exercise and choose a new person as you move through various phases of this journey.

Support Yourself with a Quote or Mantra

Developing your boundaries may be complicated at times, especially when other people don't understand your decisions. Of course, it feels good when others understand and support your boundaries, but boundaries are unique and very personal. There will undoubtedly be times when it's difficult for other people to understand your boundaries. At times like those, when external support is missing, turn inward to encourage and validate yourself.

A helpful way to cheer yourself on is to repeat a reassuring quote or mantra to yourself. These powerful words can remind you of the important work you're doing. In this activity, you will find a quote or mantra that resonates with you to bolster you in times of self-doubt or struggle.

Tools:

Computer and printer, or a piece of paper and art supplies

Steps:

1 Identify what barriers might arise as you go about setting boundaries. For example:

- Are you afraid of rejection or others being mad at you?
- Do you feel like you have too many demands at work or at home to effectively set limits?
- Do you ever avoid setting boundaries in hopes that instead, someone else will give you permission to set them? (A common example of this is a person who gives a laundry list of their responsibilities when invited to do something. Rather than politely declining, they hope the other person will understand how busy they are and let them off the hook for the event.)

2 Acknowledge any feelings that come up when you consider these barriers, such as anxiety, guilt, insecurity, or confusion. Take a few deep breaths as you allow these feelings to arise and be seen.

3 In the future, when you feel insecure, guilty, or afraid of setting boundaries, what do you need to hear to feel comforted? (If you're stuck, it may be helpful to imagine what you'd like your boundary-setting role model to say to you.) Consider a phrase that may comfort you. It could be a popular saying, a quote, or an encouraging mantra such as "This discomfort is temporary." Or you may want to remind yourself, "My future self will thank me for this hard work." Another way to arrive at a mantra or quote is to revisit your reasons for choosing to set boundaries. You can also look online for inspirational quotes. Try not to overthink your choice. Whatever feels comforting is the right mantra for now.

4 Write and illustrate your mantra or quote, either digitally or with paper and art supplies. Once you have an image, make it your phone's wallpaper to keep encouraging yourself. You may also choose to hang this image somewhere in your room or office. When you need reassurance to set boundaries in the face of difficult situations or emotions, repeat your encouraging quote or mantra.

Reparent Your Inner Child

Reparenting is a type of therapy that allows you to heal any wounds you may have experienced growing up. In this type of therapy, you learn to provide yourself with the things that may have been missing in your childhood. A healthy parent should affirm, nurture, and set boundaries to protect their child:

- **Affirming** from a reparenting perspective means providing yourself with unconditional encouragement, compassion in the face of mistakes or challenges, and reminding yourself of your unconditional worth and that no matter what, you are "enough."
- **Nurturance** refers to addressing your literal and emotional needs—for example, a safe home, weather-appropriate clothes, and a loving hug.
- **Setting boundaries** includes looking after your internal and external limits, both practical and emotional. For example, a healthy parent teaches a child how to use respectful language toward others and how to protect themselves by looking both ways before crossing a street.

In this activity, you'll assess what reparenting needs you might have and how to address them.

Tools:
Piece of paper and a writing utensil (optional)

Steps:

1 First, let's address affirmation. How does affirming yourself feel currently? Do you struggle to believe in yourself, or does this come naturally? If it doesn't, notice with compassion that you may not have had someone who affirmed you growing up even though you deserved this. Notice whatever is true now and write it down if you'd like.

2 If affirming yourself is challenging, consider your vision of your future self (from the Write the Story of Your Future Self exercise earlier in this chapter). Notice how after developing better boundaries, your

relationship with yourself is naturally more loving and supportive. How can you support and affirm your inner child acting like your future self?

3 When you consider nurturing yourself, do you find that this comes easily? Do you have a safe place to live or a retirement fund? If you practice self-care such as taking regular walks or baths, this is also nurturance. If you struggle to nurture yourself and instead neglect your self-care, validate that you may not have received examples or role models of this growing up. Maybe your mom always criticized you for being "lazy" when you rested, for example, and now you struggle to give yourself a break. You do not need to criticize anyone for a lack of guidance here. You can simply notice a need to cultivate this skill now.

4 How do you want to nurture yourself in the future? You may need to sleep more or update your wardrobe. Brainstorm or write down anything that comes to mind. Did you start this book knowing there are areas in which you already set boundaries? If so, where? Are there times maybe you weren't giving yourself enough credit? For example, you may assert yourself more than you thought. Also notice that it's completely understandable to discover that you have more work than you anticipated—or feel overwhelmed by this process. If so, can you see any places in your life growing up that you didn't receive guidance on boundary setting? Maybe your dad always complained about being taken advantage of at work, for instance, but never did anything about it.

5 Affirm all the work you have done already toward developing your ability to set boundaries. Notice the activities you have done in this chapter to strengthen your commitment to set boundaries as needed to protect yourself consistently. This is healthy reparenting in action!

Connect with Your Inner Child to Reduce Guilt

Many people feel guilty or selfish when they need to set a boundary. To overcome this common barrier, it's helpful to imagine yourself as a child. This visual allows you to imagine that you are then setting boundaries for someone else—a child who needs your help. This may help with your commitment to self-protection while lessening feelings of guilt and shame.

In this activity, you will begin to connect with your inner child—a representation of your younger self who is both joyful and spontaneous while naturally needing protection. Try to keep an open mind during this exercise even if it feels cheesy, strange, or silly. People often want to avoid the things that will be most healing to them. Allow yourself the space to experiment with all the concepts in this book to find what truly helps you.

Tools:
Childhood photos
Piece of paper and colored pencils or markers
Glue or tape

Steps:

1 Find a picture of yourself as a child and attach it to a piece of paper. (If you don't have any photos of yourself growing up—or it's too painful to look at them—draw a picture of yourself as a child like you would have when you were younger. Use your nondominant hand to draw this picture to help it look more like a child's artwork.)

2 Under or around the photo, write down information about this child as if you are speaking to someone else about them. What compliments would you give? How would you describe this child's personality? What makes this child happy? What scares this child? What are this child's favorite activities?

3 Consider how this child deserves to be protected with healthy boundaries. This can look like limiting time with the person who overwhelms this child. Or you could protect this child's health by beginning to leave work earlier. Note: If you struggle to believe this child deserves protection, please take time to contemplate this further. You may have had experiences growing up that obscured the truth of

your innate value—for example, if you were bullied, you might have low self-confidence. If you still struggle to believe in your worth after contemplation, you may want to consider therapy to address it.

4   Place or hang your photo (or hand-drawn picture) somewhere you will see it frequently, such as your nightstand or near your computer.

5   When you feel guilty about setting boundaries in the future, look at this picture. Consider this child's needs and remind yourself that you are the only person in the world capable of setting the boundaries necessary to protect this child.

More on Inner Child Work

For some, connecting with the inner child may be relatively easy. For others, it may be more challenging. If you find it difficult, take a break to practice self-care, such as taking a walk, enjoying a bath, or calling a friend. If you feel like this type of work could be helpful for you, you might consider asking a therapist for help. Besides re-parenting therapy, other therapeutic models such as Internal Family Systems draw upon the idea that you can heal by dialoguing with different parts of yourself.

Write a Goodbye Letter to Unhelpful Patterns

Sometimes letting go of old habits is a good way to make space for new habits you want to adopt. In this case, you want to learn to set boundaries, so you'll want to release any old behaviors that prevent you from doing that. For this exercise, you will work on formally saying goodbye to any behaviors that make you feel stuck or powerless.

Tools:

Piece of paper and a writing utensil
Fireproof plate and a lighter, or a small shovel (optional)

Steps:

1 Begin by setting aside about twenty minutes of uninterrupted time in a comfortable place to write your letter. This step alone is an act of boundary setting!

2 Brainstorm a behavior you want to release. You may name it directly or give it a nickname. Feel free to use your imagination. On the paper, write down what this pattern is and let it know it's time to say goodbye.

3 In the next part of the letter, validate why you acted this way—it does make sense when you consider your life experiences! Acknowledge how this behavior may have served you in the past but that it's no longer helpful. Allow yourself to feel any emotions that arise, such as anger, sadness, guilt, or grief. You can even acknowledge these emotions in the letter.

4 Next, identify any steps you will take moving forward to get rid of the old habit or move toward a new one.

5 Clearly say goodbye one last time to the old habit.

6 Breathe deeply and release this pattern. Then decide what to do with the letter. You can burn it safely in a fireproof place, bury it in nearby soil, or tear up your letter and recycle it. Here's a sample:

Dear Second-Guessing Myself,

I'm letting you go because I'm tired of feeling confused and anxious. I understand why you entered my life. Growing up, my parents always told me I was "too sensitive" so now it's hard to trust my feelings. It's exhausting to always second-guess myself.

When I doubt myself, I don't leave relationships or situations even when they hurt me, and I don't think that's the best decision anymore. I usually like to stay in my comfort zone and question if things are really *that* bad, and I'm ready to make a different choice now.

I'm ready to be free of you. From now on, when you pop up, I'm going to think about what I'd say to my best friend. Would I think she's too sensitive if she's upset? No! I'm giving myself the same support now.

Goodbye, Second-Guessing Myself!

You Have Choices

Even after you have said goodbye to this behavior, the urge to act in this way will still occur. That's okay! You will now be equipped with an idea on how to make a different choice. This awareness empowers you to choose the previously brainstormed new action rather than feeling stuck in the old way of reacting.

PART 2

Protecting Yourself

In Part 2, you will focus on protecting yourself with healthy boundaries. These include both internal limits, which ensure you are safe for yourself and others, and external limits, to protect yourself from others. You will start by honoring your right to protect your thoughts and dreams. Violations of your reality will be explored as well, in order to recognize how to fully own your reality and protect yourself from manipulation.

You will also set boundaries to protect your time, your health, your body, your work, and your finances. This is the part of boundary setting that many people initially want to skip over or rush through because of a sense it's not the "real reason" they're cultivating boundaries. Yet learning how to protect yourself is the foundation of all other boundary-setting work. You cannot have healthy relationships with others until you learn how to have a healthy relationship with yourself. Boundary setting cultivates self-love through the practice of self-protection. Over time, through this practice you will naturally doubt or minimize your needs less often.

This part asks that you give yourself time to truly hear yourself. All people have the basic need for space to process what does and doesn't work for them, which is how their boundaries become clear. Of course, at this stage of the boundary-setting journey, it's natural to sometimes want others to tell you what you need to do to be happy. This book will support you by showing you how to look within to discover what matters to you.

CHAPTER 3

Protecting Your Thoughts and Beliefs

In this chapter, you will learn about the type of boundaries that are often overlooked yet essential for your well-being: those you set around important personal concepts like your thoughts, beliefs, opinions, perceptions, identity, and intuition. In addition, these boundaries protect your beliefs regarding religion, sexuality, and politics.

These boundaries often take time to create and implement, because they affect so many areas of your life. In this chapter, you'll learn how to avoid second-guessing your opinions, respect others' right to differing views, and acknowledge anything that negatively impacted your identity. You'll also learn to identify signs that your boundaries around your thoughts are too porous. This information will help you conduct the first set of exercises in this chapter, which focus on being understanding toward yourself as you engage in self-reflection. The remaining exercises are designed to help you get in touch with your reality, validate it, and be more empowered in the face of manipulation.

Benefits of Boundaries Around Thoughts and Beliefs

When you have healthy boundaries around thoughts and beliefs, you own your opinions and perspectives without guilt or shame. Yet you also have flexibility allowing you to change your mind and update your viewpoints as needed. Taking care of your boundaries in this area is a little like being a gardener:

- You plant seeds of supportive thoughts, like you did in Chapters 1 and 2.

- You practice accepting your thoughts or beliefs that are neutral, such as whether you prefer the beach or the mountains, or your favorite type of music. This is akin to accepting the natural environment of your garden, such as the landscape and the climate. Here you are working *with* your innate nature rather than against it.
- Finally, you work to weed out unhelpful thoughts you may have. This is a form of self-protection and the practice of deciding what comes in and what stays out of your garden. You can also weed out others' version of your reality, such as their unsupportive beliefs or expectations that hurt or hinder you.

Subjective versus Objective Truths

As you build healthy boundaries around your thoughts and beliefs, you'll need to honor the difference between subjective and objective truths. These will come into play as you meet your own needs and respect others' decisions.

- **Objective reality** is the facts, such as what someone literally said, or the statement that humans need sleep to survive.
- **Subjective reality** is each person's perceptions, preferences, and feelings.

When people have differences in their subjective realities (perhaps related to having different core values), both parties should honor their truth while respecting the other person. When differences arise, a person can practice healthy external and internal limits by staying mindful of dialectical thinking. (As a reminder, dialectical thinking is when one or more things that seem like opposites can be true simultaneously.) This technique allows you to stay respectful and to compromise, because you know that each person has the right to their beliefs and they don't have to match yours.

A person with healthy boundaries avoids trying to control others' subjective realities, as this would be an external boundaries violation. For example, some religions forbid tattoos, meat eating, or abortion; some do not. On a large scale, whether it's as a country or a family, it's essential to respect your own right to your beliefs while simultaneously respecting others' right to the same. This concept will be explored further in Chapter 8.

Overcoming Second-Guessing to Own Your Identity

A person still learning how to set boundaries often struggles to know and own their authentic truth. They may feel guilty or embarrassed to have different preferences, thoughts, or beliefs than those around them. They may also struggle with self-doubt and not trust their insights, emotions, or intuition. This pattern of second-guessing often leads to anxiety. In fact, many people who are dealing with anxiety struggle with trusting themselves. Once they learn to trust their own thoughts and beliefs, their anxious feelings might lessen.

Self-doubt can also manifest as a pattern of giving others the benefit of the doubt. Believing others over yourself is a sign of porous boundaries because you cannot prioritize your self-protection if you give others the power to decide what you should think, feel, or do. Of course, healthy relationships involve listening to others and integrating their feedback as is appropriate. However, here the first step is to listen and trust yourself, *then* explore what the other person needs or wants. For example, if your partner tells you that you're being defensive, you may notice that you are trying to stand up for yourself. Yet you may also then consider that perhaps you can assert yourself while also being gentler toward your partner. Without the first step, you may feel guilty for ever doubting others and be quick to blame yourself for issues in a relationship. This tendency makes you more susceptible to gaslighting, which is when another person attempts to manipulate your thoughts and feelings.

Boundaries Keep You In Touch with Yourself

When a person struggles with boundaries around thoughts and beliefs, they may also be "out of touch" with reality. Common examples of being out of touch with your reality are trying to deny how burnt-out you are in a job or relationship. When this happens, a person may work to suppress or minimize their truth, such as thinking, *It's not that bad that I have to work overtime again.*

Refusing to accept reality, or being in denial, can have many harmful effects on your relationships, finances, and even your mental and physical health. Healthy boundaries around reality allow you to check and accept facts even when they are inconvenient or painful, such as a relationship being abusive or a chosen career being inauthentic. Ignoring your reality can be a form of self-betrayal and self-sabotage. You protect yourself when you set boundaries around what you wish to be true versus what is real.

How Your Childhood Impacted Your Thoughts and Beliefs

The experiences you had growing up, both positive and negative, helped shape your boundaries around reality. If you had parents who expected you to have the same beliefs as them, this expectation hampers your ability to create and maintain your own beliefs. This situation commonly happens with political, cultural, or religious beliefs. If you grew up in a family with strong beliefs passed on through generations, you may have a hard time identifying your authentic self as an adult. Or you might feel guilty or "bad" for having your own individual perspectives.

Another area of childhood that can impact adult boundary setting is autonomy. Parents who try to solve their child's every problem surely mean well, yet they rob the child from an opportunity to learn to effectively make decisions and trust themselves. If you grew up with the sense that you couldn't make your own choices or mistakes, you might find it difficult to set your own limits now. It is common for people with this experience to defer to others.

Parents who refused to admit to mistakes or expected perfection also impacted your current sense of who you are, your identity. This is because you may mistakenly believe that when you are imperfect or problems arise in your life, something is wrong. In reality, all people are flawed—it's the nature of being human—and problems will arise in every person's life simply because they are alive.

Finally, growing up in a home with alcoholism, addiction, or abuse can greatly affect a child's sense of both objective and subjective realities. In these families there's often a lot of secrecy and gaslighting present, such as telling children that certain abuses or violations didn't really happen or weren't that bad. When these children grow up, they often question their sense of reality and it's common that they don't trust themselves. They were told they couldn't trust their eyes, ears, or feelings by their caregivers, which wounds their relationship with their own insights and intuition.

Acknowledging these childhood experiences is not meant to attack, blame, or criticize your parents or family. Rather, this reflection helps validate why you may, at times, struggle to trust yourself. Have compassion for yourself as you develop your boundaries around your thoughts and beliefs. In the following exercises, you will work on cultivating more self-compassion, letting go of unhelpful thoughts, and honoring yourself more deeply.

Overcome Doubt and Ask for What You Really Want

You have a right to your own thoughts, beliefs, and requests, but do you ever temper how you communicate them to avoid seeming like you are "asking for too much"? This mindset leads you to avoid setting effective boundaries. In this exercise, you'll interrupt this common pattern with self-compassion.

Tools:
Piece of paper and a writing utensil (optional)

Steps:

1 Think of a boundary that you second-guess or minimize. This may be any limit you can identify with any person. For example, maybe you are worried that if you ask for more time with your partner you're being "needy."

2 Imagine a close friend or loved one telling you they want to set this limit, but they feel uncertain. Your loved one is afraid they're asking for too much or are being unreasonable. Take a moment to picture this conversation in your mind. (If you struggle with visualization, write out what this conversation might sound like.)

3 How would you respond to your friend or loved one? Would you shame them for their needs? Or would you validate this limit? Consider how you would encourage and support them.

4 Now imagine giving yourself this same support. This is the practice of self-compassion. Remember, all people need things from others—this is the natural state of humanity. There is no shame, weakness, or cruelty in having others meet your needs, wants, or limits.

5 Cheerlead your right to set this boundary by telling yourself these same supportive things you told the loved one.

Assess a Boundary by Checking with Your Intuition

A common boundary violation around thoughts and beliefs is the idea that you must trust only what's most logical and practical. However, you have an innate wisdom within you—your intuition. Learning to hear and honor your innate wisdom is an essential component of boundaries work. Only your deepest self knows your authentic emotions, needs, wants, and values. Learning to hear your personal truths reveals the boundaries you may need to set—which no one else can discover for you.

In this exercise, you will familiarize yourself with your internal guidance system—a.k.a. your intuition—by observing your body's physical cues. Learning to slow down and listen to your body allows you the space to hear your intuition. Have you ever noticed how your body reacts when something feels off to you? Maybe your stomach has turned to knots, your heart has sunk, or your throat has tightened. What does your body do when something feels right? You might automatically breathe a sigh of relief or release muscle tension naturally. This visceral sense of what is right for you is innate. Yet many people are trained to devalue or altogether stop listening to their intuition. When you learn to listen to and respect your intuition and physical sensations that accompany it, you'll discover you almost always know the best steps for you.

Steps:

1 Sit comfortably and take a few deep breaths. Imagine pulling this breath into your gut. Continue to breathe into your gut to stay connected to your body.

2 Now consider a boundary you want to set. Ask yourself, *Is this boundary right for me?*

3 Continue breathing while noticing your body's reactions. If you notice that you feel relaxed and open, this could be your body and intuition's way of saying yes. Alternatively, some people feel or hear a "yes" or "no" in this exercise.

4 Accept however your internal guidance system communicates with you. This is your truth. Try not to minimize or deny any truth that arises. This is a common reaction, especially if your intuition is revealing something uncomfortable or inconvenient. Practice hearing yourself

without rejecting yourself. Just allow it to be, rather than feeling you must act.

5 If your muscles tighten, your heart beats uncomfortably fast, or you experience a "no," go deeper. Is this reaction due to a fear? Allow yourself to sense what is true for you. You may also ask, *Is there a different boundary that will help me more that I can set?* Allow yourself to be curious as you intuit a "yes" or "no." Keep asking questions to gather more information.

6 After you listen to your body, you may be ready to set that boundary. If not, though, that's fine too. Simply connecting to your intuition more deeply is meaningful progress and worth celebrating on its own.

List People Who Influenced Your Identity

Throughout your life, you have picked up messages about boundary setting. Some messages were probably supportive, but others could have hindered your ability to be assertive. These messages can make you feel guilty, bad, or ashamed about your needs and limits. When you consciously identify these messages, you are empowered to leave them behind and instead focus on beliefs that support you.

In this exercise, you will think about the people or groups who influenced you most growing up, and what messages they passed on to you. Be sure to hang onto this paper for the next exercise.

Tools:
Piece of paper and a writing utensil

Steps:

1 On your piece of paper, make two columns. In the left-hand column, list all the influential people and environments you experienced growing up. These may include your parents, church, teachers, and coaches, amongst many more.

2 In the right-hand column, write down any specific messages that person or environment passed on to you. Don't worry about justifying or verifying these points; this only needs to *feel* right. For example:

- *Mom always did everything for us. She never sat down to eat when dinner was ready, and her food was always cold. I learned I'm a bad mom and selfish if I take any time for me.*
- *My 7th grade art teacher frequently praised my drawings. This helped build my confidence in myself as an artist even when my parents told me I shouldn't bother pursuing art.*
- *At church, I learned you're supposed to turn the other cheek. I should be the bigger person if people mistreat me and ignore it rather than setting boundaries.*
- *When I was a kid, I was bullied for being different. Now I believe I'm supposed to always agree with everything to be accepted.*
- *Dad would hold grudges. I learned that it's better to make people happy because I can't stand it when others are upset with me.*

- *My grandma left my abusive grandpa when I was growing up. This showed me it's never too late to take care of yourself or live the life you want.*
- *I learned I should be able to do everything on my own when my parents focused more time and attention on my siblings.*
- *My mom encouraged me to sing and use my voice. I learned that I have a right to be heard.*

3 Now consider whether any of these messages impacted your sense of having the right to set boundaries. Not all of them may have—just notice what's true for you. Here are some examples:
   - *When I was bullied, I figured there was something wrong with me. I'm lucky to just have people in my life. If I set boundaries, I'll probably be rejected.*
   - *Even though I know my siblings had more needs than me physically, I still think deep down that I'm not as lovable or worthy as them.*

4 Provide yourself understanding like a loving friend or parent as to why you may struggle to set boundaries at times. What would you say to a friend if they felt embarrassed about their lack of boundaries, but you knew about these experiences and messages?

Embrace Dialectical Thinking

As you complete this exercise, remember dialectical thinking. Dialectical thinking honors that two, or more, things that seem like opposites can be true at the same time. You might have loved a person and still picked up some messages from them that now hinder your ability to set boundaries as an adult. You are not attacking anyone with this list; you are simply bringing awareness to your current beliefs.

Push Out Old Thoughts and Invite New Ones In

Clarifying what has hurt you is an aspect of therapy as it allows you to perceive your options. Once you know what beliefs you have that are unsupportive, for example, you may set internal limits to cultivate more helpful thoughts. This is a feature of many therapy modalities including Cognitive Behavior Therapy (CBT), Dialectical Behavior Therapy (DBT), and Eye Movement Desensitization and Reprocessing (EMDR).

In the previous exercise, you identified the messages that have wounded your ability to assert yourself. Now you will take this awareness to create authentic beliefs which are empowering for your boundary-setting journey.

Tools:

Your list from the List People Who Influenced Your Identity exercise
Piece of paper and a writing utensil

Steps:

1 Refer back to the list of messages you picked up that interfere with your ability to assert your boundaries. On a piece of paper, create four columns. In the first column, write the name of each person or environment on your list. In the second, write the childhood event that led to a message about boundaries. In the third, write down what message you took from that childhood situation. Leave the last column blank for now. Here's an example:

My mom	Mom always did everything for us. She never sat down to eat when dinner was ready, and her food was always cold.	I learned I'm a bad mom and selfish if I take any time for me.	

2 Sit in a comfortable place with your list. Visualize yourself in the bubble explained in the Visualize Your Boundaries exercise in Chapter 1.

3 Ask yourself if the beliefs in the third column of your list feel aligned with your authentic truth. Check in with your internal guidance system—your gut and intuition—to sense a "yes" or "no."

4 If the belief aligns with what you truly think, write this message down again in the fourth column as what you believe. An example is *I believe I have the right to be heard.*

5 If this belief isn't aligned with your authentic truth, or isn't consciously what you want to keep thinking, gently cross it out and ask yourself, *What do I want to believe instead?* See what more helpful, supportive beliefs come up—trust that you know what's right for you. Write these down in the fourth column. For example, if you crossed out *I have to do everything by myself* in the third column, you might write *I believe I can ask for help and that it's a sign of strength to do so* in the fourth column. If you feel stuck deciding if a belief is authentic or not, take your time. Allow yourself space to consider newer, more helpful thoughts.

6 When you have a new belief in mind, visualize pushing the unhelpful, old belief out of your bubble. You can visualize this old belief as a color, smoke, or anything else that feels right to you.

7 Once releasing the old belief feels complete, see your new belief outside of your bubble. It could look like a ball of light or anything else. Remind yourself that you decide not only what you keep *out* of your bubble but what you allow *in*. Visualize pulling this new belief into your bubble and reality, or use a physical movement such as slowly beckoning with your arms or pulling energy down from the sky.

8 How do you feel physically and/or emotionally when you have allowed in your new, more supportive belief? Notice you may feel lighter or relieved.

9 Practice this exercise for every unsupportive and more helpful belief you've identified.

Practice, Practice, Practice

There's no failure in needing to repeat this practice over and over again. It takes a lot of time and conscious effort to allow new, more supportive thoughts to be automatic. If an old, unhelpful belief comes up again, remember you have a choice on what belief systems you nurture and cultivate. Practice pushing this belief out of your bubble as many times as necessary. Keep this practice up—it's worth it.

Verify What You Read Online

Each day a tremendous amount of information comes toward you via various types of media. When you have secure boundaries around reality, you are mindful of what is factual and what is altered, untrue, or not real. This process protects your mental and physical health from exaggerated marketing claims and information meant to manipulate your emotions. In this exercise, you will practice setting these boundaries.

Tools:
Electronic device with access to a social media platform

Steps:

1 Search social media for a topic that interests you related to mental, physical, or relationship health.

2 Find a post featuring a statistic or tip that you find intriguing.

3 Look for clues on where this information came from, such as a linked article or book. If there is no source, copy the information in a search engine to see what results and sources appear.

4 Attempt to confirm the validity of this information via multiple independent and reputable sources while setting limits on any potential disinformation campaigns or exaggerated marketing claims.

Example:

I searched ADHD on *Instagram* and found a post saying "50–75 percent of women with ADHD go undiagnosed." I then went to the website mentioned, which cites an article from the magazine *ADDitude*. In this article, a survey is mentioned where 85 percent of teachers and more than 50 percent of the public believe girls are more likely to go undiagnosed for ADHD. I then searched for the researchers' names mentioned in the article, Patricia Quinn, MD, and Sharon Wigal, PhD, in *Google Scholar*. In the journal abstract, the same numbers related to people's *sense* that girls go undiagnosed are provided. Yet this doesn't provide an objective fact that "50–75 percent of women with ADHD go undiagnosed." The social media post is really referencing the survey, rather than any true study.

Avoid Making Assumptions about People's Actions

When you have healthy boundaries around your thoughts and beliefs, you can differentiate facts, or objective reality, from subjective truths. When things are objective truths, they must be accepted. When there are subjective truths at play, however, it's important to practice accepting your own views while respecting others'.

Subjective reality highlights that while you can observe what others do or say, you don't always know their intentions. Many of us try to mind-read others' intentions or make assumptions about their actions when we don't know their personal truth. While this attempt to understand others without communicating with them is completely understandable, it also hurts relationships. Each of us can only truly know another's truth by asking them and listening to their answers. Here, you will shift from this natural urge to assume others' subjective realities to being more curious and open-minded. This practice cultivates healthy external boundaries around others' subjective realities to protect your relationships.

In this exercise, you will practice being safe for both yourself and others by respecting different subjective truths.

Steps:

1 Think of a time when someone's actions bothered you and you didn't know their intentions. For example, let's say your husband walked away when you were talking to him. You did observe him walking away; that is an objective fact. But you don't know *why* he did that—that's the subjective piece.

2 Do you notice yourself assigning a meaning to his actions? For example, you may think he walked away intentionally because he was upset or didn't want to talk to you. Ask yourself how a relationship is impacted when you try to interpret others' intentions.

3 Try to clear your mind of your interpretations. You could do this by practicing mindfulness, such as by focusing on your breath.

4 If it's a close relationship, you may want to take things a step further and communicate your interpretations or feelings, along with a request to understand him and his actions better. Be sure to validate his response— he has a right to his own interpretation of his actions. For example, you

might say, "I notice you left the room when I was talking earlier tonight. At first, I was worried I had upset you, but I wanted to talk to you before I assumed that. Do you remember why you left the room earlier when I was talking?" If he says he was distracted (rather than upset), validate that you understand he got caught up in his thoughts.

Honoring Different Viewpoints

Subjective reality also includes people's right to have different opinions. You have the right to your truth and others have this same right. Healthy relationships involve the right to engage in respectful open dialogue that may influence one another's viewpoints, while honoring each other's differences. It's an external boundary violation to try to convince others to think the same way you do.

Set Limits on Gaslighting

Gaslighting is the attempt to manipulate objective truths through various confusing tactics. For example, a person might tell you what you see, hear, feel, or know is wrong. They may say "I never said that" or "That never happened." They may mock you for being "crazy" or accuse you of doing what you know *they're* doing, like cheating. They may say you are too sensitive, and they were only joking.

In this exercise, you'll find four steps for dealing with gaslighting. Please know it takes time to develop clarity over when you're being gaslighted, but you will learn some key information here.

Steps:

1   **Trust your gut.** You will often sense when another person is manipulating you. Listen to your body and trust yourself. This is your greatest asset.

2   **Validate your truth—but don't try to make others believe it.** Remind yourself that you deserve healthy boundaries around your experiences. You're the expert of your own body, mind, and heart. When you are being gaslighted, there's a natural tendency to want to convince the other person of your truth. Yet fixating on getting others to understand or agree with you are internal and external boundary violations. When you have healthy boundaries around reality, you accept you have a right to your truth and don't need to defend or justify yourself. If someone doesn't believe you, they don't believe you.

3   **Protect yourself.** Instead of trying to convince the other person of your truth, focus your energy on protecting yourself. You may do this in various ways, including:
    - Take time away from the person.
    - Practice deep breathing.
    - Journal to validate your reality. Write out what you know to be true.
    - Consider your options.
    - Imagine yourself in a bubble, as described in the Visualize Your Boundaries exercise in Chapter 1. Now visualize yourself pushing the other person's manipulations out of your bubble.
    - Verbally set boundaries on gaslighting; for example, by saying:

- "You have your perspective and I have mine. I hope you can respect these differences."
- "You're trying to take control of the narrative."
- "I'm going to trust myself and explore my options."

4 **Celebrate yourself.** The more you act on your sense of being gaslighted, and things work out for you, the more confirmation you have of the wisdom of your gut knowing.

What Is Medical Gaslighting?

A medical professional minimizing or denying a patient's knowledge that there is something wrong is medical gaslighting. They may say the pain is in the person's head or not real. Research shows this happens more to women and People of Color. Trust yourself, find a doctor who truly listens, and keep reporting your experience.

Avoid Catastrophizing

Cognitive Behavior Therapy (CBT) is a highly effective—and widely used—type of therapy. A fundamental component of CBT is how a person's thoughts often make their problems worse. One way that can happen when developing boundaries is something called catastrophizing. This is when you imagine the worst-case scenario as highly likely or probable. When you think in such a way, you will understandably resist setting the boundaries you need because you will overestimate how poorly the interaction will go. You may fear ruining the relationship or being hated for setting boundaries, for example, when you catastrophize. In this exercise, you will begin to manage catastrophic thinking to help you assert yourself.

Tools:
Piece of paper and a writing utensil

Steps:

1 What's a boundary you are nervous to set and with whom? Write it down in the middle of a circle on the paper. Draw straight lines coming off the circle.

2 What do you fear might happen if you set this boundary? Write your answers down at the end of the lines you drew off your circle. For example, you might be afraid the person will be angry at you or begin to hate you. Don't prejudge your thoughts; just write whatever comes to mind as soon as it does.

3 How does this type of catastrophic thinking make you feel? For example, you may feel anxious, stressed, or guilty. Write your answers in the blank spaces around your circle and lines. Ask yourself, *When I think in this catastrophic way, am I more or less likely to set my boundary?* You may be understandably less likely to assert yourself.

4 Now flip over the page and in the top half, list all potential outcomes for setting this boundary with the person in mind. Let yourself brainstorm freely. Be sure to consider neutral options.

5 Review this list of potential outcomes for setting your boundary. Did you identify the *best* thing that could happen? If not, please add that to your list. Let yourself feel hopeful or excited about the possibility that setting your boundary may go well—that's a potential outcome too!

6 On the bottom half of the back side, brainstorm how you would cope if the worst thing actually happened when you set your boundary. Remember, you have survived difficult things before. If this worst case did happen, you could survive this too. (If you need self-soothing tips, explore Chapter 5.) Also remember that when you set a boundary, you discover how safe or unsafe a person is emotionally for you. For example:

- If your boundary is rejected, you will realize that this person isn't trustworthy after all. Notice you can cope with this disappointment and that ultimately, this insight is a gift.
- If the person is mad at you, notice you've been mad at people you care about before, and the relationship has continued.

7 Review your potential outcomes and repeatedly remind yourself that the worst-case scenario is not the most probable outcome.

Prepare Yourself

Remember, you can prepare to help your boundary-setting conversation go well. You could journal what you plan to say in advance so you are kind and respectful. Or you could role-play the conversation with a friend. If you need support with assertive communication, please see Chapters 8 and 9.

Practice Radical Acceptance

You can change or influence some things in life but not others. People often seek therapy when they feel anxious, depressed, or stuck trying to change things or people they cannot. On the surface, this may not appear to be a boundaries issue, but it is, because when you have healthy boundaries, you accept that you cannot change other people. In this activity, you will practice an invaluable skill to help you accept reality to be safe for you and others: radical acceptance. This is the skill of fully accepting reality for what it is. The phrase "It is what it is" is radical acceptance in action. This is a life-changing skill but is very difficult to practice, especially in relationships.

Tools:
Piece of paper and a writing utensil

Steps:

1 Take a moment to write down the parts of your life you want to change. Most people have a wound they want to heal, a habit they want to change, and/or a relationship they want to improve.

2 If you want to improve a relationship, write down in what specific ways. For example, maybe you want your mom to be less critical of you or your friend to be less flaky.

3 Review your list and underline all the situations you have complete control over changing. This may be items like finding a new job, going back to school, or learning to assert yourself.

4 Now circle anything on your list that involves other people's actions. For example, if you want your mom to be less judgmental, she'll have to agree to work on this. Take a deep breath and remember that you have the right and responsibility to assert your needs and limits clearly and kindly—yet you cannot decide if other people will change or not.

5 To get some experience with radical acceptance, practice this skill at less stressful times. Set a reminder for yourself on your phone or in your planner to "Practice Radical Acceptance" every day this week at a specific time. Choose a time in your day when you have a break and can think quietly for a few minutes. When you see this reminder, keep it in mind to work on accepting the things you can't change or control. If you encounter traffic or there's a line at your lunch spot, your natural and understandable urge may be to get upset—yet you cannot control these things. You will only add to your suffering if you get worked up about it. When these types of opportunities to *radically accept* reality arise, take a deep breath and repeat, "It is what it is." Then consider what options you have now. If you're stuck in traffic, you may have time to catch up on a podcast you like, for example.

Everyone Makes Their Own Choices

Early on in the boundary-setting journey, people commonly believe the reward for being courageous and assertive is the other person's automatic agreement to change. Yet others have the right to decide what does and doesn't work for them—just as you do. It's important to practice radically accepting their choice.

Manage Perfectionism

Healthy boundaries allow you to have a supportive relationship with yourself because you are able to set limits on thoughts or actions that hurt you. A common way people violate this boundary, however, is with perfectionism. In this activity, you will set limits on any patterns of perfectionism you may have in order to avoid unrealistic expectations and instead have a loving relationship with yourself. By shifting your thoughts away from perfection and onto learning and discovery, you are setting a boundary that can help you focus on any positive changes and improvements.

Tools:

Picture(s) of a role model or idol—this can be cut from magazines or digital
Piece of paper, poster board, or virtual board such as *Pinterest*
Writing utensils

Steps:

1 Identify your role models or idols. They may be people you know, like your parents, or famous athletes, authors, or singers. If possible, find photos of these people and create a paper or digital collage.

2 What are the qualities you admire about them? Take a moment to honor their amazing qualities, then write them near the person's photo.

3 Now take a moment to consider their flaws, struggles, or difficulties. These may be easy to identify, or it may be challenging. If you find yourself thinking that they're "perfect," notice that this idea isn't based in objective reality. All human beings are imperfect. You may admire a singer for being brave, creative, and wealthy, yet notice they also have struggled with mental health issues. Of course, you shouldn't judge these flaws or difficulties negatively—the point is to notice that no one's life is "perfect." Add these notes near the person's photo alongside their other qualities. You can also include words, phrases, or quotes that represent your role model's strengths and difficulties to remind you of their humanity. This helps set limits on thoughts that some people, especially those you may admire, are "perfect" or never struggle.

4 Practice radically accepting that you're perfectly imperfect, just as every other human being is. Notice that perfectionism is a distortion of reality, as no person is capable of being perfect.

5 While you work on accepting that perfect is a lie, you can set limits on feeling like a failure. Shift your thoughts from what you failed at to what you're discovering. Learning what does and doesn't work is important information that helps you reach your goals! Celebrate any progress. You can also validate why you may not have made "progress" yet. Maybe you're overwhelmed or scared. Don't judge yourself; simply notice.

CHAPTER 4

Protecting Your Time

The boundaries you set around your most precious resource—your time—are some of the most important. These intentional limits allow your daily life to reflect your values and priorities. Your routines and schedule can align with your authentic wishes, allowing you to live with meaning and integrity.

So many people nowadays feel drained, exhausted, and overwhelmed by the demands of their lives. Yet when they realize they need boundaries, they feel guilty implementing them because they feel so obligated to their many responsibilities. While it is understandable to struggle with setting these boundaries, you will be much better off once you do it. Setting boundaries around your time helps you account for your responsibilities *and* your free time. We all have obligations, but we also all deserve to enjoy unscheduled time to relax and recharge.

This chapter will help you understand where your time is going, set limits on your availability, and set and communicate boundaries around your time.

Stop Putting Off Your Happiness

Time is one of the few things in life you cannot buy or bargain for more of. Yet in a culture that praises productivity and doing as much as possible, pushing back on requests, invitations, and demands can feel exhausting and isolating. But you are sacrificing your health and happiness with this packed schedule. You might want to do x, y, or z to improve your well-being, but can't because you are "too busy." Do you envision a future reality where you will have the time to do the things you want and be happy? It's time to stop putting that day off—you can jump there now by using boundaries.

Setting boundaries around your schedule ultimately provides you with more peace and more time. When you have healthy boundaries around your time, you can make choices about how to spend your days according to your values, goals, energy, or mood, rather than procrastinating or going to events you don't really want to attend.

Challenging Prevailing Narratives about Time

Setting boundaries around your time is complex because you must also challenge long-standing narratives in your personal and professional life. For example, you might believe that saying no to a request is lazy or impolite. You may struggle with boundaries around your time if you grew up with your time being overly controlled or structured. As a child, you might have been taught the importance of sacrificing all your time, money, and energy, which can make you feel guilty about setting boundaries later in life. Or, perhaps you are now a parent who feels bad for wanting time for themselves. Some of these narratives are deeply engrained in various cultures, adding another difficulty in developing these boundaries.

The workplace is another area that has unrelenting expectations about your time. Though workplace managers often say they care about work-life balance, many only give lip service to real boundary setting. The company leaders might say they want employees to value time off, but then they still expect the employees to be available constantly. Or they may offer counterproductive help, such as requiring employees to spend precious time attending a workshop on preventing burnout. Exhaustion and "bragging" about working more than forty hours a week are commonplace and celebrated. Given the common contradictions, many people understandably fear setting boundaries with work because they worry their career will suffer because of it.

The truth is, boundaries are vital to your health and well-being. Whether the boundary around your time is related to personal relationships, parenting, or your job, it's worth setting even in the face of going against society's norms. *Not* setting boundaries around your time can easily lead to burnout and mental or physical health issues.

Remember, you deserve to experience the fullness of life alongside meeting your responsibilities.

Can You "Have It All"?

The concept of "having it all" is a contentious one. Some people say that you cannot, while others insist it's possible. The key problem in this debate is "all-or-nothing" thinking—that if you can't do everything you want, you're a failure. It's very common yet unhelpful, as this type of thinking typically keeps people stuck and confused.

Instead, the truth is more nuanced—you might be able to have many experiences, but not all at once. For example, you cannot simultaneously be a digital nomad while creating deep, long-term roots in a community. You cannot simultaneously have the freedom of being childless while experiencing the rich emotional reality of being a parent. Life offers many rich, diverse, and contradictory experiences—take part in what's important to you at this moment! Your priorities may change over time, allowing you to shift to a new experience. At any given time in life, you can have all that is most important to you. You can live a rich, satisfying life you are proud of by prioritizing your values. This is done by setting boundaries around your time.

Prioritizing Time Based on Your Values

When you are connected to your values, you live in a way that promotes genuine peace, joy, and pride. Values are your life's priorities; the things that allow you to live a meaningful life. Your values, like your boundaries, are personal and unique to you, and could include things such as family, health, having fun, or the environment.

It's easier to prioritize your time when you "schedule" your values, as they point to where and how you want to spend your days. We'll explore your values in this chapter so you can start putting them front and center as you consider how you spend your time. From there, you can build a realistic schedule for yourself, learn how to say no gracefully, and truly enjoy the present moment.

Challenge the "I Have No Time" Assumption

Each person is allotted the same amount of time each day. If you don't set boundaries around that finite time, you may understandably feel as if you have none, because it's being drained away as you do things you don't want to do. Boundaries act as a sturdy container for your time. Without them, your time may feel like it exists in a bucket filled with holes. This is a stressful way to live as it may feel like you are always overwhelmed and exhausted.

When considering setting boundaries around time, a common automatic response is "I have no time." This is an especially common response when someone wants to take time for something fun, such as spending time with friends. In truth, saying "I have no time" is a telltale sign that you need to set boundaries around your time! In this activity, you will challenge this thought by tracking how much time you are spending on screens. The information you gather will help you reorganize your time and reduce stress and pressure on your schedule.

Tools:

Electronic devices you frequently use: your smartphone, tablet, laptop, TV, etc.
Preferred app that tracks your usage time, such as Clockify for your computer and App Usage for your phone
Piece of paper and a writing utensil, or a digital notepad

Steps:

1 Download apps to track your usage on each electronic device you use. You will be tracking both your personal and work-related usage of these devices to highlight how much total time is spent on your electronics. Some apps will automatically work in the background to track your usage; others you have to open up when you want to use them. Commit to using these apps throughout the next seven days.

2 For any devices you can't track electronically (for example, if you have an older-model TV), record the time you spend on it on a piece of paper or on your phone for seven days. Simply note the day and how many minutes or hours you used the device.

3 At the end of the seven days, collect the totals in one place, on a piece of paper or on your phone. For example, you might write that you spent

ten hours watching TV, ten hours on this app, eight hours on another app, fifty hours on your work computer, and so on. Estimate where necessary—perfect accounting is not the goal.

4 Consider if any of these activities or apps may be a "time vampire" that has been draining your most precious resource without you even realizing it. Star any categories that you might want to make a change around.

5 Decide what boundary or change to implement around your electronics, if any. For example, a small step might be to use an app for thirty less minutes next week, while a drastic step would be deleting an app off your phone entirely. You might choose not to change your work computer usage at all. Note: There is no need to take action if you're not ready—your awareness and contemplation is enough.

Don't Judge
Try to refrain from judging your screen time or activities. There is no shame in screen time, nor do you have to defend or justify why you were using any device or app. Stay open-minded and compassionate, and use this exercise just as a learning experience.

Identify Your Values

When asked one's values, people usually list the things they think they "should" value. Yet these may not be your true top values—and this is completely okay. In this exercise, you will identify your real personal values so you can begin to plan your time around those values and establish boundaries to protect them.

Tools:

Your future-self visualization from the Write the Story of Your Future Self exercise in Chapter 2 (optional)

Your anchor word from the Build Hope with an Anchor Word exercise in Chapter 2 (optional)

Sticky notes

Piece of paper and a writing utensil

Steps:

1 Make a list of your authentic values on a piece of paper. To help spark ideas, try these suggestions:

- Think about when you visualized your future: What were you prioritizing? These priorities provide insight into your values. You may value adventure if you saw yourself traveling, for example.
- Consider your anchor word. This may highlight a value of yours—even if you're not yet fully living this way. If you chose peace, for example, you may value emotional stability or healthy relationships.
- Imagine you had more space in your schedule. What would you do with it? Your answer may highlight a value. If you want more unstructured time, you may value freedom. Or if you saw yourself cooking, you may value health or creativity. Notice what resonates as your values.

2 Narrow down your list to your top 3–5 values. Write each word on its own sticky note and hang them somewhere visible so you can be reminded of them every day.

Identify Where Your Schedule
Is Out of Sync with Your Values

Feeling guilty is a sign that something's not in sync between your actions and your values. Identifying the root of that imbalance will allow you to make adjustments to address it. Many people feel guilt in relation to their schedule and how they spend their time.

In this activity, you will identify an area of your schedule where your values and actions might not be aligned. As you explore your imbalances, please give yourself grace. There is no shame or weakness in being out of sync—everyone experiences it from time to time. You are showing great strength by becoming self-aware of these moments so you can address them.

Tools:
Piece of paper and a writing utensil

Steps:

1 Consider your daily schedule. Do any events or moments make you feel guilty? If so, they might be violating your values. Write down whatever comes to mind—that is the right answer to explore currently. For example:

- You may value your family, yet notice that at night, you're so exhausted from trying to keep up with all your demands that you zone out on your phone instead of talking to your children.
- You may value mental health but overschedule yourself to the point of feeling scatterbrained and forgetting to practice self-care.

2 Once you are clear on an area of your life in which you are violating your own values, take several deep breaths in and out. It takes a lot of courage to notice where you are making choices that aren't in alignment with your genuine values, so celebrate this progress. The next exercise can help you make the necessary changes to better align your schedule with your values.

Create a Routine Aligned with Your Values

Setting boundaries around your time entails not only what you want to say no to but what you want to say yes to as well. Each time you set boundaries around your time, you are saying yes to creating more of the future reality you want.

In the last activity, you reflected on the times you are doing something that feels out of sync with your values. Now you will begin to implement changes to create an authentic routine.

Tools:

Your list from the previous Identify Where Your Schedule Is Out of Sync with Your Values exercise

Piece of paper and a writing utensil

Steps:

1 Use your intuition to brainstorm a few small changes you want to make to your schedule, especially as it relates to any values you are not currently honoring fully enough.

2 Think small: A new five-minute routine that you can stick to is infinitely more valuable than a large change you cannot maintain. You can change your entire life by making a series of small changes over time.

3 Write down what internal and external boundaries you may need to implement these changes. You may have to let your partner know that you will need to watch a little less TV at night to go to bed earlier (external). Or you may need to set internal limits; for example, to not check work emails after dinner and instead take a walk.

4 Now decide whether you need to communicate this small change to your schedule to anyone else. If you want to take more time to wash your face at night, you may want to let your partner know that you are creating a new routine. Or if you want to stop calling your mom on the way home from work because you need some quiet time, you could let her know you are making this change. List any people you need to contact.

5 Now consider what you need or want to say. You are not asking for permission (that would be a porous boundary)—you are simply sharing

your goals and changes as a courtesy to them. If you need support with asserting yourself, please read or review Chapters 8 and 9.

6 Implement one, some, or all of these small changes to your schedule, depending on your comfort level.

Awareness Is the First Step

Developing a schedule to protect your values may feel intimidating or overwhelming at first. That's perfectly understandable. If you don't feel comfortable making any changes yet, be patient and try again in a week or two. Over that time, remind yourself that when your schedule is aligned with your values, you're more likely to be happy, calm, and fulfilled. Bringing your awareness to this truth can help you gradually accept it.

Turn Off Phone Notifications

With smartphones, it may feel like people have constant access to you and your time. All those notifications, buzzes, and chimes demanding your attention create stress. Furthermore, notifications interrupt your ability to focus on your priorities. In this activity, you will take action to set limits on your smartphone to protect your time.

Tools:

Your smartphone

Steps:

1 This exercise is really simple: Turn off all notifications in the settings of your phone. If you feel comfortable, you may do this from now on. However, if intense uncomfortable feelings arise, try doing this for a full day at first. Continue this practice of detoxing from notifications once a week until you feel comfortable increasing the frequency.

2 Now let's deal with the resulting feelings that arise—likely guilt, a sense of obligation, or fear of missing out. Allow yourself to notice these. Take a deep breath and notice where these emotions may be in your body. Move your body as you feel is right if needed. For instance, you may want to roll your shoulders or neck if you notice tension there.

3 Can you support yourself with a cheerleading mantra? Consider statements that feel empowering, such as "I feel uncomfortable about this change but that's okay. I am safe to evolve." Or you may affirm that you are in charge of when you check your apps on your phone—not the device or apps themselves.

4 If turning off some notifications isn't possible for your work, ensure you turn off all others that are optional. When you are not contractually obligated to be available to work, turn off your work notifications. It may feel tedious to keep changing the settings, but you are protecting your time, energy, and attention. You make boundaries work easier for yourself when you change these environmental distractions whenever possible.

5 If turning off notifications such as those for your texts isn't possible or you don't feel ready, try keeping your phone in another room when it's not needed, such as when you're cooking dinner or talking with roommates or family members.

Say No to a Request

When setting boundaries around your time, you must say no to some requests. Yet commonly, people feel guilty wanting, or even needing, to say no. They may think they should do as much as humanly possible. Or they may feel afraid that others won't like them if they say no. This creates a vicious cycle in which people betray themselves to please others. Eventually, this cycle can lead to burnout, depression, and overwhelming anxiety.

Other times, a person with porous boundaries might be able to say no, yet feel compelled to provide an endless list of reasons as to why they must decline. You have the right to say no without justification. In this activity, you will practice being truthful about your limits with others.

Tools:
Mirror

Steps:

1 Think about a time someone said yes to you when they should have said no. You will know if, say, they canceled at the last minute for another event (e.g., an appointment they forgot). Or if the other person expressed resentment over doing this task for you. They may have expressed this as a guilt trip, such as saying you need to help them move because they took you to the airport.

2 How did it feel to be on the receiving end of another person's lack of boundaries around their time? Likely you felt anger, confusion, or shame over being resented, guilt-tripped, or canceled on. Notice how saying no with honesty and clarity is actually a loving option even if it feels difficult in the moment.

3 Consider an upcoming event that you are dreading, such as a holiday celebration, an overtime request, or a social gathering.

4 Listen to your body. Your sense of dread is your intuition telling you this request is too much for your current amount of time or energy— or is not aligned with your authentic self. Sometimes, we don't want to do something because it isn't aligned with our values. Other times, it's because our schedules are overpacked and we are exhausted. Notice what is true for you. Validate that it makes sense why you don't want to do this.

5 Practice saying no (without apologizing!) to this request in the mirror. Try to make your response as succinct as possible. If you overexplain, you risk potentially overwhelming the listener. You could offer to meet up with someone on another day or to help out with a different request— but only if it feels authentic to you, not out of guilt or obligation. Practice being honest and genuine in your "no" rather than placating the other person. Again, you have the right to say no and this honesty is the foundation of healthy relationships! Here are some examples of what you could choose to say:

- "Thank you so much for inviting me but I won't be able to make it this time. I hope it goes wonderfully, though!"
- "I notice I'm already scheduled for something else that day."
- "I appreciate that you want help that day but unfortunately, I'll be unavailable."

6 Cheerlead yourself with a positive mantra. Think about what your boundaries role model (from the Find Your Boundary-Setting Role Model exercise in Chapter 2) would say to support you.

7 Communicate with the person, either directly or via text if you don't feel ready for an in-person conversation. Feel the emotions that arise, including anxiety and guilt as well as relief, courage, and pride.

8 Celebrate yourself—you can do this even by exclaiming "Yes!" to yourself, playing a game you like, dancing, or bragging to a friend—this is a huge accomplishment!

When You're Questioned

Sometimes, people will try to convince you to say yes or they will question your "no." Let them know that you appreciate that they value your presence or support, but restate that attending isn't an option. (You may also then disengage from the conversation, e.g., saying you will be working the rest of the day, to prevent further back and forth.) If someone asks why you're saying no, and you feel comfortable sharing, feel free to say something like, "I'm really trying to keep a closer tab on my time lately to be more present with my family." Alternatively, you have the right to say no and the right to not explain or justify yourself.

Prevent Resentment with Self-Care

Resentment is always a sign of porous boundaries. This resentment arises if you don't honor your own needs or set the boundaries you need around your time. Then you wonder when you will get a break—when someone else will see how hard you are working and give you time to yourself. In this situation, you are both looking for others to read your mind and waiting for permission to set boundaries—and you now know that isn't the way to approach limits. In this activity, you will set limits around resentment.

Tools:

Piece of paper and a writing utensil

Steps:

1 Signs you feel resentful include thoughts of "What about me?", "When will I be recognized?", or "When do I get my needs met?"

2 First, write down a list of areas of your life where you feel resentful. It's sometimes uncomfortable to acknowledge resentment, but you can both love someone deeply and resent them at times. Furthermore, being honest about your resentment allows you to become more authentic and loving.

3 Write down what thoughts or feelings are beneath your resentful thoughts. What do you wish you were receiving? This may be acknowledgment, time to yourself, or rest, to name a few examples.

4 The only way to interrupt the cycle of resentment is for you to set an internal limit. You will stop feeling resentful when you find a way to give yourself what you need, rather than waiting for someone else to give it to you. You get a break when you give yourself a break. Find one way to begin to interrupt your resentment now. This might look like talking to your partner about needing some time alone on the weekends. Or it could mean ending work at a certain time or celebrating an accomplishment. Whatever ideas come to mind are right—trust yourself.

Respect Others' Time

Boundaries around time also include how you treat other people's schedules. A common way you may, unintentionally, be violating others' boundaries is by wanting to control how they spend their time. Thoughts that someone "should" be available to you or make time for you highlight this type of boundary violation. If you have a pattern of repeatedly texting people until you get a response, this is also a sign that you are trying to control their time. Some partners want to dictate when their partner cleans or how they spend their social time with others. Other people have a natural urge to control the time of their employees, coworkers, children, friends, or family. You may genuinely believe your preferred schedules or ideas are better for them. However, others have the right to make their own choices about their time.

In this exercise, you will reflect on any areas where you might be violating others' boundaries and work to change that behavior as needed.

Steps:

1 Explore if there are times in your life you may be controlling—or attempting to control—how others spend their precious resource of time. Practice self-compassion as you reflect. Trying to control others' time is a natural response to fear. Validate why you are afraid in this situation. If you want to prevent your partner from going to a bachelor party, for example, you may be afraid they will cheat.

2 Explore where you need to set limits on yourself to respect others' time. If you're a parent, this is nuanced. On one hand, it is part of your job to structure your child's schedule and routines such as when they go to bed. On the other, if you are overscheduling them—you'll know because they will tell you how tired they are—you may need to practice setting a boundary. Be gentle with yourself—it is hard to detach from controlling others' time. Practice talking to yourself like a loving parent or as your boundaries role model would.

3 Consider what you can do with the time you give yourself back when you let go of worrying about others' schedules. What would you want to do instead of controlling others' time? See if you can start practicing this activity. For example, instead of trying to spend all your time with

your best friend maybe you'd love to go to a yoga class alone. Or maybe you want to release dictating what your partner makes for dinner on their night to cook and take a bath instead.

4 Practice respecting the other person's time by choosing to do this other preferred activity instead. If you need to schedule it in advance, like a dance class, do so now. Otherwise, block off at least fifteen minutes the next time you would have the opportunity to violate the other person's time, e.g., if your partner cooks dinner on Tuesdays, block time off for your bath on this night.

5 If you are struggling to release control, be patient with yourself. This is a complex skill that takes lots of practice! To support yourself, practice visualizing how the other person may feel to have some space. How may they think or feel? Notice the relief or appreciation they'd likely feel. Take a moment to imagine how *you* will feel when you choose to do something you'd like instead of feeling obligated or compelled to control the other person's time. Picture what it'd be like to give yourself this time and space to read, take a bath, nap, or do any other activity you want instead. How will your body feel when you choose to do this activity? What emotions will likely arise? Finally, as you focus on yourself and respect another person's time, how do you think this will impact the relationship? What positive effects might you notice?

Controlling versus Inviting

Controlling time is not the same as wanting to spend time with someone. Asking a friend to go to the movies when it works for both of you is healthy. Control is trying to dictate that your friend meet you at 5 p.m. for dinner and then go to the 7:30 p.m. show near your house, for example.

Focus On Only the Present Moment

You might be spending a lot of your precious time ruminating about the past or worrying about the future. That habit is likely to create anxious or sad feelings and not really resolve anything anyway. To feel more peaceful, it's important to learn to let go of overthinking about either the past or future. You can do this by focusing on the present moment—in other words, practicing mindfulness. You are also setting limits on an often-overlooked time vampire—too many thoughts about the past and future.

Steps:

1 Take a deep breath, bringing air into your belly. Slowly exhale through your mouth. Becoming aware of your breath is a simple and effective way to practice mindfulness. Your breath can only exist in the present moment.

2 Take another breath. When you breathe in, say to yourself, "Breathing in, I breathe in." Notice what it physically feels like to take this breath in through your nostrils and into your lungs.

3 Exhale through your mouth. When you exhale, say to yourself, "Breathing out, I breathe out." Notice the breath leaving your lungs and your mouth.

4 Repeat this practice for another four breaths, again saying the statements. Try to allow your breath to become deeper each time.

5 Repeat this practice whenever you find yourself overly focused on the past or future.

Embrace Boredom

When developing meaningful boundaries around time, you might experience an internal conflict. You probably know that taking time for yourself would help, but you might also feel guilty about it. It's only with a lot of practice setting boundaries that people can honestly say, "I had a lazy day without guilt!" This isn't the first stop on the journey to setting effective boundaries around your time. Initially, the goal is to take time to rest and relax even while feelings of guilt, anxiety, or boredom arise. This activity will help you practice taking short amounts of time to yourself, even if you have nothing planned.

Tools:
Piece of paper and a writing utensil

Steps:

1 Find a quiet space and set a timer for sixteen minutes (this gives you a moment to get settled). This may mean you have to wake up earlier or go to bed later if you live with other people. Alternatively, you may do this in your car.

2 Hide your phone in a drawer or bag.

3 Get settled in a comfortable spot quickly. Now do nothing for the next fifteen minutes.

4 Accept that this exercise may be uncomfortable or boring. If the exercise is boring, that means you're doing it correctly! Research shows boredom reduces stress, improves focus, and increases creativity. Still, it can be scary to just exist. Feelings or thoughts that you have tried to avoid might come up in the silence. These may include resentments or limits you need to set. Allow yourself to honor any anxiety that may arise at the thought of just being. Feelings of guilt may also arise. Notice if any of your values validate the need for space and time to yourself.

5 You will likely have the urge to get up, check something, or pick up your phone. Try to resist these urges and focus on your breath as you did in the Focus on Only the Present Moment exercise if you'd like. Keep breathing and interrupting your urge to be done with this exercise or distract yourself as needed. This is the practice of mindfulness in action. It can be very uncomfortable and challenging to cultivate this skill, but it's tremendously important work for your life in general and boundary-setting skills specifically.

6 When the timer goes off, turn it off and get up.

7 Take a moment to freewrite about how this time to yourself felt. Were you bored? Guilty? Thinking about all the other things you "should" have been doing? Notice with compassion that these are emotions and thoughts that prevent you from setting boundaries around your time. Jot down whatever comes to mind.

8 Congratulate yourself. It takes courage to allow yourself to just be!

CHAPTER 5

Protecting Your Mental Health

Setting boundaries to protect your mental health is an essential part of becoming—and staying—emotionally regulated. Emotional regulation refers to the ability to manage your emotions effectively using various coping skills and strategies. When you are emotionally regulated, you are able to honor what you feel in a balanced way and thoughtfully respond rather than automatically react to your feelings. Initially, being emotionally well regulated may not appear to involve boundaries; however, they are a critical component of all mental wellness.

To effectively set boundaries with others, you must learn to cope with uncomfortable emotions in healthy ways. For example, you'll need to learn to manage feelings of guilt, anger, resentment, and self-doubt. Coping well with your emotions is an act of self-respect and self-love. It's also an act of love and respect for others, because you are able to be clearer and kinder with others even when setting limits with them.

The activities in this chapter will teach you to become more aware of your feelings. This is especially useful if your mind goes blank when asked to identify your emotions or if you have a pattern of denying your emotions in favor of helping others avoid pain or feel better. You will also practice accepting your right to all your emotions—you don't need to minimize or hide what you feel. Finally, you will practice newer, healthier ways to cope in order to care for your mental health consistently.

Learning the Basics of Emotional Regulation

We all have some way of coping with our emotions. The problem is that many of us have learned counterproductive ways, which may help in the short term but only make things worse in the long run. You know this if you have over-eaten to try to feel better when you were upset or bored…but then you felt physically uncomfortable and perhaps ashamed or self-critical afterward.

There are better ways to face difficult feelings. This process relates to boundaries because when you process your emotions in a healthy way, you become more emotionally regulated. As you become more regulated, you then are better equipped to set additional boundaries you need. This creates a positive cycle in your life because as you continue to set boundaries, you feel greater peace and confidence as situations that currently hinder you improve.

Undoing Unhelpful Habits

Throughout your life, you have likely picked up messages, either consciously or unconsciously, about your emotions. These messages may have told you some of your emotions are "good" or "unacceptable" or "bad." These messages are further complicated by toxic positivity, which is the promotion of the idea that it's not okay to feel painful or uncomfortable emotions. People then who are truthful about the range of their feelings are seen as "killing the vibe" rather than accepted for being honest about the human experience. The truth is that there are no "bad" or "good" emotions.

It is normal and natural to experience the entire range of human emotions in your lifetime. This includes joy, love, and excitement but also grief, rage, and despair. You have the right to feel every and any emotion. Of course, emotions such as happiness or hope are generally comfortable to feel, while others are uncomfortable. (Some people feel uncomfortable with joy, however, typically out of the fear that it won't last. This can be a sign of unresolved trauma or depression.) It's best to think of emotions as information that is guiding and enriching your life.

Let Your Emotions Out!

Many people struggle to validate and accept their emotions because they have digested these messages that you shouldn't feel some emotions. You might then either deny your emotions—especially the ones that are uncomfortable or that you may judge—for example, by thinking, *I have a great life; it's ridiculous for me to feel sad.* Or you might unconsciously suppress the difficult feeling, or do things such as drink alcohol to push the feelings down. Unfortunately, while completely natural, the urge to hide or deny emotions always creates further problems. For instance, if you deny your anger with someone, you will leave the emotions unprocessed and neglect to set a necessary boundary. Then later you may find yourself yelling at this person over "nothing."

Trying to hide or deny your emotions, especially anger, is ultimately destructive. While you may be able to stop yourself from exploding at others, your anger could also be turned inward, toward yourself. This often manifests as symptoms of depression, such as not wanting to get out of bed in the morning, experiencing hopelessness, or always feeling tired no matter how much you slept.

Avoiding Mental Health Boundary Violations

Just as you want to set boundaries that work for you, it's helpful to be aware when your own boundaries are being violated. A person with porous boundaries around their mental health sometimes struggles in their relationships due to a pattern of overempathizing with others. Empathy, with healthy boundaries, is an incredibly uplifting emotion that can nurture your relationships with others. Without healthy boundaries, however, empathy can become self-destructive, leading someone to neglect themselves and be filled with anxiety-inducing self-doubt. Here are some rights you can maintain as you take care of your boundaries:

- **You have the right to your feelings *and* the right to not take on others' emotions.** In fact, to be safe for others, you must provide them with space to feel, and cope, with their own feelings. This will be explored in the activities of this chapter.
- **You have the right to privacy around your feelings.** You have the right to decide what, when, and how much vulnerable information you share with others. Of course, like a flexible bubble, this will differ depending on your closeness to the other person.

- **You have the right to feel whatever you feel.** Common boundary violations when it comes to your emotions and mental health are being mocked about your feelings such as being told you're "too sensitive" or "dramatic." If someone is telling you what you feel isn't right or proper, that is a form of gaslighting.

As you become more adept at processing your emotions, you'll feel more confident protecting these boundaries and exerting your rights.

Accept Whatever You Feel

To cope well with your emotions and set the boundaries you need, the key is to practice validating—and accepting—your right to all your feelings. Coping well with your emotions allows you to respond rather than automatically react to your emotions. For instance, when you feel anxious, you do not need to give into the automatic urges of avoiding, withdrawing, or procrastinating. You can feel afraid to set a limit with someone, and still choose to be courageous rather than ignore the problem. Responding wisely to your emotions not only protects your mental health; it often protects many other aspects of your life, including your relationships.

There are many ways you may choose to cope well with your emotions. You may already have healthy ways you cope at times with your emotions—sometimes it's helpful to think of these as your coping skills "toolbox." Some examples of coping skills are taking deep breaths when you feel uncomfortable, using aromatherapy when you're anxious, taking a walk to clear your head, calling a friend to get support, or playing a game when you need a fun distraction.

Feel Your Feelings

A common issue, especially early in therapy or for someone just beginning to learn emotional regulation, is saying "I don't know" when asked what you feel. This may not seem like a big deal, but it's very difficult to cope well with something you're not aware of feeling. Not knowing how you feel is a symptom of emotional disconnection from yourself, and often leads people to react emotionally—like snapping at their partner—and not even knowing where this reaction came from.

If you tend to always be working or "on the go," you may find you are disconnected from your emotions. Or, if you focus on caring for others' emotions—and trying to make them happy—over your own feelings, you will naturally be detached. This exercise will show you how to connect more deeply with your body to help you identify your emotions. Learning to identify your emotions—and proactively care for them—is a major step toward being a safe person for yourself and others.

Tools:

Piece of paper and a writing utensil

Steps:

1 Your body and its sensations will often clue you in to how you are feeling emotionally. Some people commonly report feeling certain physical sensations for their emotions. For example, your stomach may wrench when you feel guilty or your heart may ache when you're sad. Are there any clear physical signs you have for intense emotions? Jot down a list. Building this self-awareness helps you become more mindful. The next time you feel your jaw tighten, for instance, you may ask yourself if you are stressed, angry, or maybe both.

2 Take a deep breath. Now, scan your body mentally. Explore if you feel any physical sensations right now, and whether they are comfortable, neutral, or uncomfortable.

3 If you notice a physical discomfort such as shoulder tension, take a breath, focusing on this body part. Keeping an open mind, ask yourself if this discomfort is tied to an emotion. If you hear a response—perhaps that headache is caused by stress and anxiety—send appreciation to

your body and intuition for sending you this message. Write down what you learn. Allow yourself to trust whatever responses come to mind. There is no wrong answer, and your body has an innate wisdom related to your emotions. If you struggle to hear anything from your body, this is not a problem. Allow yourself to remain curious as you make a practice of checking in with your body. Wherever you are with this exercise, practice being compassionate, gentle, and understanding toward yourself. It's understandable to be disconnected from your feelings sometimes!

4 Now that you have more awareness as to what you are feeling, literally and emotionally, explore if there are any healthy ways you can cope. If you are anxious, for example, maybe you can practice deep breathing or go for a walk outside.

Understanding Dissociation

Complex trauma (which includes ongoing neglect or abuse) and severe accidents can lead to something called dissociation. This is a more extreme form of disconnection from your feelings in which you may not feel truly here in your body, or you may feel like a floating head. It is completely possible to heal from complex trauma, but it's outside the scope of this book. If you experience dissociation on a regular basis, please seek therapy. If that's really not possible, research shows developing a yoga practice—which you can do for free—may meaningfully reduce traumatic symptoms.

Identify Unhealthy Emotional Processing Habits

Most people have times when they cope with their emotions in unhelpful or even harmful ways. This is natural and completely understandable—especially if you never learned how to cope with your emotions effectively growing up. Setting limits on unhelpful coping strategies is one of the most important boundaries you can set to protect your mental health.

In this activity, you will identify a harmful behavior you sometimes turn to when you feel upset, and learn how to replace this behavior with a healthier choice that's more effective. The process of replacing unhelpful, or hurtful, coping strategies with kinder, more effective strategies takes time and practice. Please be patient with yourself.

Tools:
Piece of paper and a writing utensil

Steps:

1 Divide your piece of paper into three columns. Label the first one Coping Mechanisms, the second Results, and the third one New Choices.

2 In the first column, list any ways you cope with your emotions that create further issues. Common examples include gambling or unnecessary spending, binge drinking or eating, abusing prescription medications, or spending time with people who make you feel used. Don't judge your actions; simply notice these habits.

3 In the second column, write down how these behaviors cause further problems for you. If you shop when you are sad, you may go into debt, for instance. If you identify any behaviors or urges that threaten your survival, like increasing drug abuse, highly restrictive eating, or thoughts of suicide, please seek professional support. It may literally save your life. You are worth it! This is the most important boundary you may ever set with yourself.

4 Review your first column, and star one of these behaviors to practice setting limits with.

5 Reflect on the emotions that may lead you to act on the urge. For example, loneliness may cause you to hang out with people who are disrespectful. Or you may binge drink when you are bored, lonely, or

angry. Whatever emotions seem to trigger this behavior for you are valid. Be sure to practice self-compassion for all pain you identify. You are acting in a way that's unhelpful because you are trying to survive difficult emotions. Try to release shame as you honor your own suffering. You deserve kindness rather than judgment for how you are reacting to your pain or suffering.

6 Now use the third column to brainstorm more supportive ways that you could cope. Perhaps you could call a good friend who lives far away instead of meeting up with closer friends who aren't kind to you. Perhaps, if you are lonely, you might consider getting a pet. Or you may take a walk or attend a workout class instead of going to happy hour.

7 Practice mindfulness to stay aware of when the emotional trigger for this urge and behavior arises. Try to turn to the more helpful strategies you already identified or others that you think of later. Imagine telling yourself no to the hurtful urge, like a loving parent would. Encourage the more helpful coping skills instead.

Radically Accept Your Emotions with a Mantra

Radical acceptance is the willingness to accept reality for what it is. (You can visit the Practice Radical Acceptance exercise in Chapter 3 for a general activity on this topic.) "Reality" involves the wide range of human experiences, from minor inconveniences to tragedies like natural disasters. This is a coping skill you can practice anywhere—you only need your thoughts. Radical acceptance is *not* the same as saying you agree or are happy about the reality. It's the acknowledgment that denying reality never changes reality. Instead, rejecting reality only adds to your suffering. If you radically accept it's raining, you will still be wet. But if you reject this reality, you will be wet—and upset.

There are no "bad" or "wrong" emotions. Experiencing the wide range of emotions is part of the human condition. Recognize that how you cope may be helpful or unhelpful, but these urges are not a reflection of the emotion itself. This activity will guide you on how to reframe the idea that some emotions are "wrong" and practice radically accepting whatever feelings arise for you.

Steps:

1 Take a moment to acknowledge that you have the right to feel every, and any, emotion. In fact, your emotions are an important source of information your body is sending you. When you judge—or don't want to feel—certain emotions, you're missing a valuable opportunity.

2 Think about a challenging situation you are in. What are you feeling? Try to identify every emotion, including the ones you feel an urge to judge. For example, you might think, *I'm sick of doing all the planning and transportation for our kids' after-school activities—my partner doesn't help. I'm saying I'm "sick" of it, but really, I feel angry, hurt, resentful, and unsupported. I don't like feeling this way toward my partner—but it's true.* Notice that these emotions exist whether you accept them or not. These are your genuine feelings—which you have a right to feel (and which have valuable lessons for you). Consider how denying or minimizing these feelings doesn't make them go away. It likely just makes the situation feel worse.

3 Take a deep breath and say, "It is what it is that I feel _____" and insert your various emotions. To carry on the previous example, you might say, "It is what it is that I feel unsupported, angry, resentful, and hurt toward my partner." Radical acceptance will be an ongoing practice for you—you will naturally reject reality again. When this happens, simply return to your mantra.

Accept the Gift of Your Anger

This exercise will go deeper toward accepting the emotion that is most essential for setting boundaries—anger. Anger is also the emotion that many people most negatively judge, which makes it a challenge to accept feeling this emotion. Most of us have picked up messages that anger is bad, wrong, or unattractive. People-pleasers tend to feel especially uncomfortable with anger.

Try thinking of anger with a new mindset: Anger is the emotion that points you to a boundary that's not being set or enforced. Whenever you feel angry—including frustrated, agitated, or resentful—toward someone or something, this is a sign of an unmet need or a boundary that's being violated. In this exercise, you'll focus your awareness on accepting anger to identify the boundaries you may need to set.

Tools:
Piece of paper and a writing utensil

Steps:

1 In the center of your page, write the word "anger" and circle it. Around the circle, write down messages you have picked up around "anger." Did you learn that it's scary? Bitchy? Powerful? Unloving? What words or actions come to mind when you think of anger—yelling? You can also write down your automatic responses to the idea of what you "should" do with anger—for example, "turn the other cheek." Just write whatever comes to mind.

2 Review the page and ask yourself if any of these messages about how to approach anger hinder your ability to set healthy boundaries. If you believe that it's "rude" to express anger—even kindly—you may naturally avoid asserting yourself. Contemplate if these messages around anger lead to other uncomfortable experiences. For example, if you ignore your anger, your feelings will fester, and you'll build resentment toward someone. If you numb your anger, you might later feel depressed and ashamed.

3 Now flip over the page and write down a more supportive perspective on anger. Maybe you want to remind yourself that honoring your anger allows you to set boundaries that ultimately protect your relationships.

4 Now contemplate a situation that makes you feel angry—this includes feelings of annoyance, irritation, rage, and resentment. Perhaps you're annoyed your sister is critical of your new relationship or you're irritated that your roommate leaves dirty dishes in the sink.

5 Consider the gift of your anger in this situation. What is your anger revealing to you about your needs or limits? You may need time, for example, to consider your feelings about your new partner before getting others' feedback. Or you may need your roommates to contribute to household chores.

6 When you accept the gift of your anger, does a boundary you need to set become clearer? Contemplate what this limit may be and write it down. Are you ready to act on it? If not, consider what other tools you may need and explore other chapters in this book accordingly.

Use Belly Breathing to Think Clearly When You're Emotional

When you feel pressured, stressed, or overwhelmed, it can be hard to think clearly and make healthy decisions. We've all had moments when we wish we had made a better choice when we were emotional. This inability to think clearly is not a personal weakness to feel bad about—it's actually a part of your body's physical reaction.

When you are stressed or emotional, your sympathetic nervous system is activated. This process helps you prepare to fight or run away in the face of danger. This nervous system response is highly advantageous in short durations, but becomes problematic when you constantly feel under stress. Furthermore, if you aren't able to effectively interrupt your fight or flight response as needed, not only do you feel bad but you may do or say things that you regret in the heat of the moment.

To think clearly and relax, you must activate your parasympathetic nervous system. This part of your nervous system is also called the "rest and digest" system. It's only in this state that you can relax, heal, and recover. Here your heartbeat slows, and you breathe more deeply. As your body relaxes, you are better equipped to feel calm enough to manage overwhelming situations in a supportive way for yourself and others. In this activity, you will learn how to activate your parasympathetic nervous system whenever you'd like.

Steps:

1 Find a comfortable chair to best support yourself in this activity. Ideally, you want to put both feet on the ground and try to sit up as straight as possible—but please honor your own body and make any modifications to this pose as needed to ensure you are not physically uncomfortable. Take a moment to breathe naturally. Then place one hand on your chest and one on your belly.

2 When you breathe in, notice which hand rises more: the one on your chest or the one on your belly?

- If your **chest** rises more, your breath is shallow. This is very common, so don't worry. True deep breathing is a skill that takes practice to do naturally. It may be helpful to practice it daily before bed to help you fall asleep. It is important to work on this skill because shallow breath keeps your sympathetic nervous system turned on.

- If your **belly** rises more, you are soothing your nervous system. This type of breathing comes naturally to some people. Having a history of swimming or playing instruments often helps.

3 No matter where your breath went, please practice the upcoming visualization to relax your nervous system:
- Visualize a balloon of any color right at the base of your lungs.
- Inhale through your nose, while imagining this balloon is expanding.
- Exhale through your mouth, allowing the balloon to deflate completely in your mind.
- Repeat this breath cycle and visualization four more times. Each time, allow your breath to pull deeper into your belly, expanding the balloon further. When you exhale, continue to allow it to deflate as much as possible.

4 Notice how you feel after these breath cycles. Many people feel more relaxed. Sometimes, spontaneous crying or laughing even occurs. Other times people feel dizzy from this increase in oxygen. If this happens, you may need to do fewer breath cycles when you repeat this visualization for a while.

5 Repeat this visualization whenever your mind feels cluttered or you feel stressed. You are helping your nervous system relax, which allows you to think more clearly.

Practice Self-Soothing

When you're really upset, it's hard to focus on the things that might calm you down. When you're emotionally distressed, your sympathetic nervous system is activated, which leads your prefrontal cortex—the part of your brain that can think through problems and make wise decisions—to shut down. Fortunately, you can plan ahead to support yourself when you are overwhelmed in the future. In this activity, you will identify self-supporting strategies to use in the future when you're upset. Having these tools ready beforehand will help make them more accessible in difficult moments.

Tools:
Piece of paper and a writing utensil
Stickers (optional)

Steps:

1 Take a moment to list all your favorite ways to calm down and feel better when you're upset or feeling bad. You may have a lot of ideas—or just a few—either is okay. Make sure these activities are truly supportive to you (rather than ultimately harmful). A few things to keep in mind:
   - Examples of these activities include practicing yoga, standing on grass, listening to music, working out, calling a friend, watching your favorite movie, reading, listening to comedians, painting your nails or doing makeup, aromatherapy, meditating, coloring, reading inspirational quotes, being in nature, listening to the sound of rain, walking your dog, listening to podcasts, or practicing deep breathing.
   - Often, the most soothing ways to care for yourself involve your senses—and if you can layer this experience, all the better! For example, taking a bath could have warm water for touch, flowing water for sound, and a scented bath bomb for smell and sight (if you use colored bath bombs).
   - It's especially helpful if these activities are accessible and don't require much planning or money.
   - Crying is another helpful self-soothing skill that's often overlooked or judged negatively. If you tend to get lost in your tears, though, you may want to set a timer to remind yourself to not get swept away in your emotions.

2 If you feel stuck coming up with activities, think back to your favorite activities as a child. You may want to add these to your list, such as playing with LEGO® bricks, going to the park, drawing, blowing bubbles, or dressing up. Remember dialectical thinking—an activity may seem silly *and* be genuinely soothing to you. Set limits on any part of you that believes there are "better" or "worse" ways to support yourself. It's okay to have fun while you care for your mood!

3 If you'd like, decorate this list with stickers or drawings.

4 Keep this list in an accessible place to remind yourself of your self-soothing strategies whenever you feel overwhelmed.

5 Feel free to add to this list over time. Your favorite strategy may differ at times depending on the situation and your specific emotion(s). You may prefer dancing when you're angry and journaling when you're sad, for instance.

Make Self-Care Easy

Take your self-soothing skills a step further by compiling items from your list (like bath bombs, tea, inspirational books, and essential oils), and putting these things somewhere accessible, like your nightstand drawer. Next time you're upset, simply reference your list, and then go to one place to find these items to soothe yourself quickly.

Practice Mindfulness to Soothe Yourself

Harvard University researchers Matthew Killingsworth and Daniel Gilbert discovered that the average person was not paying attention to what was in front of them a full 47 percent of the time. When your mind wanders, you are vulnerable to experiencing symptoms of depression, stress, anxiety, and other uncomfortable emotions. Mindfulness is a highly useful skill to cope with this distraction and protect your mental health. How does mental chatter take away from your emotional stability? These distracting thoughts could include ruminating on what others did or said that upset you. Or these hurtful thoughts may include your inner critic, who constantly reminds you of your mistakes or shortcomings. Obsessing about what may go wrong in the future is also a common unhelpful distracting thought.

Mindfulness is the act of paying full attention to the present moment without judging it. This definition comes from Jon Kabat-Zinn, a mindfulness expert and author. Often, people want to cover up their distracting hurtful thoughts with more positive ones. They tell themselves they "should" be grateful, for example, or they practice affirmations. While affirmations and gratitude are helpful practices in general, they might not completely silence the mental chatter. To interrupt thoughts that may hurt your mental health, commit to practicing mindfulness. This practice nurtures your mental health in two critical ways: It reduces your mental chatter while providing you with a self-soothing skill you can use anytime, anyplace.

Steps:

1 You practice mindfulness when you pay full attention to whatever you are doing with an attitude of radical acceptance ("It is what it is."). Your mind will wander when you practice mindfulness—now and in the future. This is not a problem. Part of practicing mindfulness is returning your focus back to what is happening in the present moment: what you are doing, how you are feeling, what you are hearing, what you are seeing, etc.

2 Pick an activity you want to do mindfully—this could be a task on your to-do list, such as folding laundry, or a self-soothing activity, such as deep breathing. You may also choose to be mindful while eating or walking.

3 Do this activity as you normally would but pay attention to your thoughts. When your mind wanders—as it will—bring yourself back to what you are doing in a neutral way. If you're washing dishes, for example, notice how the water and soap feel on your hands. Using your senses is a great way to come back to the present moment.

4 Keep returning to the present moment for as long as it takes to complete this task. It may feel tedious to keep returning your attention to what you are doing rather than getting lost in your thoughts and that's okay. Mindfulness is an incredibly helpful skill to protect your mental health but it's challenging for many of us. In fact, it's called a mindfulness "practice" because you can't master mindfulness—some moments it's easier; others, harder.

Balance Empathy and Self-Compassion

When a person has porous boundaries, they sometimes get overwhelmed by feeling other people's emotions. When this happens, they may feel lost in the face of others' problems or emotions. They may feel like they have lost themselves or their sense of purpose. They may also feel like they are living for everyone else, and their own life is passing them by. You might have heard these people called "empaths."

Caring for others' emotions reveals a great capacity to love, but it must be balanced with a focus on yourself. The questions and reflections in this activity will show you how to balance your sense of empathy for others with empathy for yourself.

Steps:

1 Ensure your bubble (from the Visualize Your Boundaries exercise in Chapter 1) is up all the way around you. This is where you are fully protected—you have the right to set boundaries for your safety and you may be flexible to negotiate with others to meet their needs whenever possible.

2 Consider whether there are any situations or relationships you feel stuck in because you're prioritizing others' feelings. Perhaps you have stayed in your hometown because you don't want to hurt your mom, or you have stayed in a job you don't like because you don't want to burden your boss.

3 Take a moment to honor the other person's feelings. List the reasons you feel empathy for them.

4 Now show empathy toward yourself with self-validation. Validation is the skill of saying that what someone thinks, feels, wants, or needs makes sense given their life experience, their personality, and/or the situation. Self-validation is when you give yourself this same nonjudgmental understanding. Tell yourself *why it makes sense* you feel this way. Notice that your feelings or concerns are completely valid. Example: It makes sense I want to move away. This town lacks the opportunities to grow my career. I also value adventure. Also, I have the right to want to move away—I'm an adult.

5 Revisit your bubble. Imagine pushing your sense of responsibility to care for the other person to the point of self-neglect out of the bubble. You may see this as smoke, shapes, or anything else. Let your intuition guide you.

6 Now imagine pushing the other person's feelings or concerns out of your bubble. You are responsible for your own self-soothing and boundary setting. They are responsible for the same for themselves. Keep moving their energy out in a way that intuitively makes sense until it feels complete. If any supportive thoughts come to mind, say them to yourself. Example: I love my mom, but it's a natural life-stage issue for her to learn how to cope with my moving away.

7 Feel the relief of balancing your sense of empathy for others with your own self-love.

Let Your Bubble Protect You

If you don't claim space for yourself and validate your feelings, you will likely be anxious, full of self-doubt, or depressed, feeling like you're walking through mud. Visualizing your bubble daily—or whenever you interact with others—helps you validate your right to have your own needs, feelings, values, desires, and boundaries. It also helps you from taking on their emotions as well.

Set Limits on Media That Upsets Your Mental Health

The media you consume, including social media, TV, news, podcasts, and books, has the ability to help or hurt your mental health. People often consume media for relaxation or to disconnect from their worries. Yet some of the media you consume may actually make you feel worse. Examining what you feed your mind and then setting boundaries to protect your mental health are key steps in making sure you are exposing yourself to media that boosts your well-being.

Steps:

1 Identify your preferred media to consume, including genres of media and platforms. For example, maybe you love the topic of cooking, so you tend to watch these types of shows and listen to related podcasts.

2 Take a moment to consider how these types of programs, books, etc. affect your mental health. Your automatic response may be to be defensive or protective of your desire for such entertainment. Honor this while being willing to really explore what your body and intuition tell you about how these types of programs impact you.

3 Are you uplifted by this media? Does it bring you down? Make you fearful? Angry? Is it relaxing? Notice what is true for you.

4 If you notice that this media brings you down or upsets you in some way, you may have the urge to justify your consumption of it. Notice that you can find this media entertaining and it can still negatively affect your mood.

5 If the media upsets you, would you be willing to set boundaries on consuming this? For example, maybe you no longer want to follow specific social media accounts that bring you down. Or if you tend to feel powerless whenever you read the news, maybe you need to set a timer when you do consume media about current events.

6 If you are not willing to set limits on this media, why not? What are you afraid of losing out on? Could you honor this fear while setting a small boundary with this limit? Maybe you don't want to stop watching true crime documentaries, for example, but perhaps you could set the limit to not watch them right before bed if it impacts your ability to sleep well.

Declutter to Improve Your Mental Health

While letting go is an important aspect of developing your boundaries, it is hard to do. You might fear if you let go of certain things or people, then you will be left with nothing or no one. Or you may think that something, even if it's not good for you, is better than nothing.

This exercise will help you learn to literally let go. Decluttering your space has many benefits, including making things easier to clean, while also potentially eliminating reminders of a difficult situation.

Tools:
Box or bag to collect donations

Steps:

1 What physical items do you have in your space that negatively impact your mood? An old mug may remind you of a previous job you hated, for instance.

2 What are the negative mental health consequences of holding on to this item? Old yearbooks may make you feel insecure, as an example.

3 What are the positive consequences of getting rid of this item? Maybe you will feel less triggered to call an ex if you get rid of a sweater they gave you.

4 Ask yourself what prevents you from getting rid of this item. Honor whatever you hear. Clinging to an item that makes you feel bad is symbolic of holding on to behaviors, relationships, or situations that make you feel unsafe or unsupported. You can recognize that this is understandable, while also knowing you can make new choices.

5 Now visualize the relief you will feel when this item is gone from your space. You will never need to be physically confronted by it again!

6 If you feel ready, get rid of the item by recycling or donating it. This courage and the willingness to let go will help you set boundaries in the future.

7 If you are not yet ready to release the item, put the item in a box and hide it away as best as possible. This is still an important step toward letting go!

CHAPTER 6

Protecting Your Body

Your right to protect your body includes limits around how you "should" look, your food intake, how and when you like to be touched, and how you take care of your body. The activities in this chapter will honor your right to self-care, help you manage any guilt about this, and keep your body safe from hurtful comments and behaviors.

An important note: Please be mindful of your needs and history, as violations including assault and abuses are briefly mentioned. If you have a history of trauma to your body and are working with a therapist, you may want to wait to begin this chapter with your therapist. If you cannot attend therapy at this time, you may want to complete—or review—Chapter 5 first. Please take breaks and use your self-soothing skills as needed.

The Benefits of Setting Boundaries about Your Body

Setting boundaries to protect your body has numerous benefits, such as:

- Nurturing your physical and mental health
- Feeling more grounded, emotionally stable, and confident
- Improving your relationships with others by helping you feel less irritable or resentful
- Improving low self-esteem since it is an active step you can take to feel more self-loving

Know Your Rights

You have many rights when it comes to protecting your body. This includes the right to decide how close others can get to your body. Remember the image of the bubble from the Visualize Your Boundaries exercise in Chapter 1. How close others get to your bubble may differ depending on the person, your mood, and the situation. For example, while you have the right to set limits on any unnecessary and unwanted physical closeness, someone may need to stand closer to you than you prefer if you're in line for a crowded show.

When it comes to your body, you also have the right to decide when and how you want to be touched. This is true no matter the other person's intentions. Having this right denied is a common physical boundary violation. If while you were growing up, you were told to "be nice" and hug people you didn't want to, this is a boundary violation. Also, it is a boundary violation if people grab, touch, or hug you without your consent.

Protecting your body also includes your hygiene and your right to seek medical care. If you experience illness, you have the right to create a plan that meets your authentic needs and values as well as to get a second—or many—opinion(s). You also have the right to seek alternatives to traditional medical care to protect your body. Then you have the responsibility to care for yourself while also respecting others' right to make their own health decisions. Finally, you have the right to protect yourself from others' judgment and comments about your body.

The Effects of Body Boundary Violations

When the right to decide how or when others touch you is violated, it can negatively impact your relationship with your body. This includes commonly dismissed violations, such as being hugged without your consent, and more overt traumas, such as physical and sexual abuse. These violations impact your sense of safety in your body as well as your ability to advocate for your physical and sexual health. (How to advocate for your sexual health, and manage any sexual pressure, will be addressed in Chapter 9.)

Any history of trauma that hurts your body naturally impacts your ability to set the limits you need to protect your body. Besides physical and sexual abuse or assault, other traumas that hurt your body include injuries, accidents, food scarcity, eating disorders, the pressure to look a certain way, and neglect, including a lack of physical touch growing up. Neglect naturally hurts a person's sense of their right to care for and protect their body.

Extreme enmeshment where a parent may have fixated on their child's body, including its appearance and/or athletic performance, often sends the child the message that they don't truly own their body. (Enmeshment will be discussed further in Chapter 8.) This situation can lead to dissociation, where a person detaches from feeling present in their body because their body no longer feels safe or actively feels like an enemy. If you experience dissociation, see a professional therapist to address it.

Prioritizing Physical Self-Care

Self-care is the practice of prioritizing actions that help you feel balanced physically and emotionally. This differs from self-soothing, which are the things you do to feel calmer when you are emotionally distressed. These behaviors may overlap but it's the intention that differs. You might write in your journal if you're angry after a fight with your partner to soothe yourself. You might also journal every night before bed to clear your head to help you sleep—that would be self-care.

You have the right to care for your body—and to take the time to do so. In fact, a key part of protecting your body is taking the time to practice self-care. Neglecting this right is an internal boundary violation. Common ways that neglecting self-care manifests in the body include struggling to get out of bed, experiencing brain fog, or feeling like you're walking through mud.

Many people avoid setting boundaries to protect their body because they don't want to be "selfish." If you have that mindset, know that self-care is one of the most loving things you can do for others. Without protecting your body with self-care, your physical and mental health will break down. If this occurs, it hurts your loved ones to see you so depleted and perhaps you would need their caretaking. If you do not care for your body, you will also inevitably become too exhausted to be truly present for your loved ones. This is not truly loving.

Keep It Simple

The practice of self-care can sometimes be overcomplicated by the media—it can look like you need loads of extra time, energy, or money to do self-care "right"— through expensive supplements, branded products, or complicated routines. To start out, just focus on your basic physical needs: movement, nutrition, hydration, and sleep. The boundaries you work on in this chapter can do wonders for your physical health and mental outlook as well.

Make Progress in Five Minutes a Day

When people want to start a self-care practice, they often overcommit themselves. Someone who doesn't currently exercise may suddenly decide they need to commit to going to the gym five days a week. Or a person may decide they need to practice multiple new habits at once, such as meditating daily while eliminating dairy from their diet. While this ambition is admirable, it often is a recipe for disappointment. To benefit from self-care, it's important to create a manageable and sustainable self-care plan. This means starting in a way that takes very little time and effort. The best plan is to pick one small thing you want to do for yourself daily and then build a habit around this for a few weeks. Once this feels natural, you can add in another small but loving activity for yourself. Or extend the amount of time you invest in the first activity by a little bit. But for now, start small and simple. This activity will show you how.

Tools:

Printed monthly calendar or digital checklist with thirty days listed

Steps:

1 Think back to a previous self-care plan or New Year's resolution that you weren't able to follow through on. Validate why it makes sense you couldn't maintain this plan. What were the barriers? For example, maybe your gym is too far away to commit to going daily. Have compassion for yourself.

2 Decide on one small thing you would like to start doing for yourself daily. Please choose an action that only takes five minutes—or less—a day. Also, this small change should not cost you anything. Here are some examples:
   - Go to bed five minutes earlier a night
   - Commit to washing your face before bed
   - Practice deep breathing at red lights
   - Stretch for five minutes before bed
   - Spend five minutes being mindful outside in the morning while you drink your coffee

3 You may need to set limits on yourself if you hear yourself saying this isn't "enough" self-care to start with. Remember: The simple self-care you can commit to long-term is infinitely more valuable than an elaborate plan that is so time- or labor-intensive that you give up.

4 Commit to this self-care practice daily. Schedule this time in your phone or planner now to remind yourself of this small activity.

5 When you complete the activity, check it off on your paper calendar or digital checklist. Cheerlead yourself! You are making tremendous progress in just a few minutes a day!

Address the Big Three: Food, Water, and Rest

Your physical body and your mood are interconnected. You are likely familiar with this if you've ever been "hangry." The "big three" physical factors—food, water, and rest—are responsible for a lot of poor moods. In this activity, you will identify how various physical states impact your mood. You will also plan around these states to improve your mood while protecting your body and your relationships.

Steps:

1 First, let's focus on **food and drink**: Do you ever forget to eat or drink enough water in a day? If so, how does this impact your mood or ability to focus? When you are dehydrated or hungry, how does this impact how you treat others or any other areas of your life? Perhaps you can't focus, for example, when you are hungry or thirsty. This lack of focus may impact your productivity at work or you may be more irritable with others. Researchers have found that even slight dehydration—only 1 percent level of dehydration—in women is enough to lower mood and lead to problems concentrating.

2 Moving on to **rest**: Do you ever have nights where you didn't sleep enough? If so, how does this impact your mood? Does being tired impact your ability to focus and the way you interact with others? When you're tired, you may perhaps snap at your kids more or feel more hopeless or overwhelmed throughout your day. Another study found that couples struggle to resolve conflict effectively and positively when just one person is sleep-deprived.

3 If possible, consider ways you can prevent some of these physical triggers for mood or focus problems. For example:
   - **Food:** I will leave snacks in my desk or purse to eat as soon as I remember this need.
   - **Water:** I will try to start my day off by drinking eight ounces of water.
   - **Rest:** I will set limits on how much time I commit to TV shows in the evenings.

4 Celebrate your insight and plan—you are protecting your body, mental health, and relationships by managing common physical triggers wisely!

Push Past False Guilt

One of the biggest barriers to taking care of your body is guilt around self-care. Often, this is not authentic guilt, though—it's false guilt. Authentic guilt arises when you violate your values. If you value honesty, you will naturally feel guilty when you lie. This guilt teaches you to make different choices to live with integrity. False guilt arises when you go against what you believe you "should" do based on messages you've internalized from society or people around you. This activity will help you explore your own guilt related to self-care and try to transform it to a different mindset.

Tools:

Your list of values from the Identify Your Values exercise in Chapter 4
Pen or highlighter

Steps:

1 Take a moment to read the following list. Circle or highlight any statement that you relate to:
  - "I shouldn't say no."
  - "Self-care is a luxury I can't afford."
  - "Other people need me too much for me to take time for myself."
  - "I shouldn't do or buy something nice for myself."
  - "I should be able to do it all. It looks like other people can."
  - "I'm afraid my partner (or anyone else) may be mad at me if I take time for self-care."
  - "I'm a bad mom (or dad, wife, husband, daughter, son, etc.) if I take time for me."
  - "Self-care is selfish."

2 Review the statements you highlighted. Did you pick up any of them from someone else, e.g., the media, your culture, or a family member? For example, you may not authentically believe you are a bad partner for taking time to nourish yourself, but growing up you heard that taking time to rest is "lazy."

3 Imagine pushing the beliefs that aren't truly yours out of your boundaries bubble (from the Visualize Your Boundaries exercise in Chapter 1).

4 Decide if any of these beliefs do feel aligned with your genuine values. You may truly feel nervous that your partner will be upset if you practice self-care because you love them.

5 Now take each belief you resonate with authentically and explore the facts. How does this belief negatively impact your body? Your mental health? Your relationships? Here's an example: *Because I believe I shouldn't do something nice for myself—and I can't afford self-care—I never bother trying to practice self-care. But then, I feel irritable and tired—all the time. I've been sick three times in the last six months. And I resent my husband when he goes out with friends because he's doing something nice for himself.*

6 Is there any way to look at this belief differently? Imagine that your boundaries role model (from the Find Your Boundary-Setting Role Model exercise in Chapter 2) is speaking to you, or that you are speaking to your best friend. Here's a sample dialogue you could have internally:

Self: "I learned that taking time to practice self-care is lazy and selfish. But I am noticing that I don't know if I entirely believe this anymore."

Role Model/Friend: "I'm so glad to hear this. It makes sense why you believed self-care is lazy and selfish given your background. But I'm glad you're questioning this. How do you feel when you ignore self-care?"

Self: "When I don't take care of myself, I tend to get sick. Then I have to take time off work and cancel plans I was looking forward to. I also tend to snap at those closest to me. I feel awful when this happens."

Role Model/Friend: "This is great to notice. You're right that without self-care your body gets depleted and your relationships suffer. Are there simple ways to start protecting your health and your relationships more with self-care?"

Self: "I notice that going to bed earlier is completely free and that if I do this, I'll wake up feeling better. When I feel better, I can keep my commitments to others. I'm also much easier to be around when I feel well rested!"

Role Model/Friend: "This makes sense. Are you willing to make the commitment to go to bed earlier—even if it's just ten minutes earlier—starting tonight?"

Self: "Yes!"

7 When your authentic guilt arises in the future, practice speaking to yourself with compassion.

Schedule Your Self-Care

People with porous boundaries around self-care often mean well—they do put self-care on their to-do list. But their self-care never makes it to the top of that list; instead they keep moving time for themselves to the "next day." This becomes a vicious cycle in which it becomes second-nature to deprioritize themselves. For this activity, you will put self-care into your calendar to make sure you actually do it.

Tools:

Your paper calendar or calendar app

Steps:

1 Do you ever feel angry or pressured by the idea of self-care? Do you feel like you already have too much on your to-do list? Validate these feelings. It makes sense you may be frustrated by the idea of doing *more*.

2 Honor the dialectic: It may feel like more to care for yourself *and* when you do this consistently you will feel like you have more time in your day. It takes a lot of time and energy to push forward when you feel drained *and* it will be worth it.

3 Practice the courage to change. Schedule a self-care activity in your planner.

4 Treat this like an appointment with another person you can't break—even if the self-care isn't relaxing yet. It may not feel that way yet if you have a lot of guilt or pressure around your to-do list. In time, you will feel clearer and calmer.

5 Stick with your commitment to yourself. You are worth it. And if you don't believe this yet, self-care will help you value yourself more.

Treat Your Body with Respect and Love

A person with porous boundaries may neglect—or actively harm—their body. They may also try to soothe and comfort themselves in ways that ultimately are harmful. Sadly, self-neglect (and potentially abuse) sends you a subconscious message that you are not worthy of care. This creates a cycle of self-neglect or self-abuse. The checklist in this exercise will help you identify areas where you may need to set limits on self-neglect and self-abuse in order to treat your body with the love it deserves.

Tools:
Writing utensil

Steps:

1 Check off the ways you may be neglecting, or hurting, your body from the following list. This list is not exhaustive in the hopes of reducing overwhelm. Feel free to add to the list and take a break if needed.
   - ❏ Forgetting to eat
   - ❏ Not drinking enough water
   - ❏ Not showering regularly
   - ❏ Restricting food
   - ❏ Binge drinking or binge eating
   - ❏ Abusing drugs
   - ❏ Forcing yourself to work—or work out—when you are sick
   - ❏ Cleaning excessively to the point of injury, aches, or arthritis
   - ❏ Working too many hours
   - ❏ Not sleeping enough
   - ❏ Having unprotected sex with partners you haven't discussed health or pregnancy risk with
   - ❏ Eating food that makes you sick for comfort

2 Take a deep breath. Just bringing awareness to these habits can be painful and overwhelming. Yet the first step to protecting your body fully is knowing where you need to set limits.

3 Validate why it makes sense you are acting in these ways. Talk to yourself like a best friend.

4 Pick one activity from the list just discussed to address for now. You may always address more later, but meaningful change happens in small steps.

5 Set limits on this harmful or neglectful behavior by replacing it with something more self-loving. Introduce this new activity in small steps if needed. If you want to work fewer hours, maybe you could choose one night a week (rather than all five) to go home earlier. If you don't want to eat foods for comfort that make you sick, you could buy alternatives of these foods, such as replacing ice cream with dairy-free ice cream.

6 Create a plan to help you with this goal. If you want to drink more water, you may keep a reusable bottle at your desk. Or if you want to go home one night a week on time, you may block off that time on your work calendar and perhaps speak to your boss. You may also make a commitment to your partner to be home for dinner together that night.

7 Find ways to hold yourself accountable in a gentle way. For example, you could set a timer to ensure you keep your commitment to go to bed earlier. Or you could make a plan to see a friend one evening weekly to ensure you leave work on time. When you choose to set limits on harmful activities toward your body, you act as a loving parent. You are nurturing an essential part of who you are—your body.

8 Be gentle with yourself. It takes time to replace old behaviors with new ones, but each time you act in a new way, you are deepening your boundary-setting skills and showing your body respect.

Communicate with Others about Your Body

A common boundary violation is when others discuss your body without your consent. This includes both compliments and criticisms. This violation may trigger feelings of anger and insecurity, or hurtful behaviors toward your own body, like overeating to "rebel."

Safety, for many people, involves protecting themselves from others' judgments and comments about their own body as well as from diet culture in general. This exercise will show you how to exert your right to protect yourself from others' judgments and comments about your body. *No matter their intentions.*

Tools:
Piece of paper and a writing utensil

Steps:

1 Think about times when this issue arises. When are others commenting on your body, either positively or negatively? Your mom may comment on your weight regularly perhaps. Or maybe you have a friend who is always comparing your bodies. Write down these situations.

2 Now write down how your relationship with your body and potentially your health are impacted by others' judgments and comments—positive and negative—about your body. You may feel pressured to look a certain way, for instance, if you get a lot of compliments about your body. This may trigger you to restrict your food. When you restrict, you may notice that you struggle to focus and are irritable. In time, restricting your food may lead to nutritional deficiencies and health conditions.

3 Contemplate how the conversations you are involved in—or exposed to—negatively impact your body image. For example, maybe your friends often discuss their newest diet or criticize their bodies. Or perhaps you follow people on social media who have what you consider the "perfect" body.

4 Write down how these conversations or social media accounts make you feel in your body. How do they impact your health? You might skip sleep to work out if you have friends who are critical of their own bodies. You

may then feel hungrier throughout your day, which naturally happens as a result of sleep deprivation. You may then overeat, leading you to feel more insecure about your body...which leads you to lose sleep to work out again. These sorts of patterns can create a vicious cycle.

5 Now let's move on to setting necessary limits. If you need to set a boundary with someone, what do you need to communicate to this person? You may ask your mom, for instance, to refrain from talking about your weight—whether it's positive or negative—as it stresses you out. Or you could ask your friends not to talk about what they hate about their bodies with you. If you need support with asserting yourself, see the assertive communication scripts in Chapters 8 and 9.

6 If you are exposed to things on social media that hurt your relationship with your body, what limits do you need to set? You may need to unfollow certain accounts. You might also want to follow people who support the relationship you want to have with your body.

7 Implement these boundaries. If you are nervous or reluctant, imagine the relief you will feel once you no longer hear or are exposed to the things that impact your ability to feel safe in your body. Consider how it will help you feel more confident too.

Nourish Your Body

Setting boundaries to protect your body includes examining your approach to food and eating. You have likely picked up messages about food throughout your life that impact your relationship with both food and your body. This may include the idea of "good" or "bad" foods, and they can come from your family, the media, your culture, and coaches.

This activity will guide you as you ask your body what it needs and listen to its answers. Please take breaks, use your self-soothing skills, and seek outside support from a therapist as needed if you have a history of disordered eating.

Tools:

Piece of paper and three different markers: a color you love, another you don't like, and a color that is neutral in preference to you

Steps:

1 Divide your paper into three sections. In the first section, write down what messages you have picked up about how you should—or shouldn't—eat. You can use any color writing utensil.

2 In the second section, freewrite about how these messages have impacted your relationship with food and how you eat. You may feel guilty eating certain foods, which makes you have "cheat days," for instance. Or you may rebel against these messages, frequently eating the foods you "shouldn't."

3 In the third section, write down how these messages have impacted your relationship with your body. Maybe you are controlling your body or you may be neglectful of it.

4 However you currently feel about food, and your body, take a moment to begin to breathe deeply. Bring loving attention to your belly. Notice that your body belongs to you. You are the expert of your own body and its needs.

5 Take another deep breath into your body and belly as you imagine your bubble around you (from the Visualize Your Boundaries exercise in Chapter 1). Push any messages you picked up about food that don't align with your truth out of your bubble. These may look like smoke,

shapes, or anything else that comes to mind. Allow your intuition to guide you.

6 Begin to connect with your body on a deeper level. Notice your body has always been here with you—ready to connect with you. If you listen, your body always has messages for you—authentic messages about your needs, including those for nourishment.

7 Flip over the piece of paper and draw a circle with your neutral color. Ask your body what foods it genuinely prefers and likes. Keep an open mind as you hear the response. Write these foods inside the circle with a color you prefer.

8 Now ask your body if there are any foods your body doesn't prefer to digest. Stay committed to hearing your body with love. Write these foods outside the circle with the color you don't prefer. Thank your body for speaking to you. Remember, you can connect with your body at any time to update these preferences.

9 Based on the information you received, is there one small change you want to make to nourish your body in a more authentic way? Think about a food you may want to add into your diet rather than remove, especially if you have a history of restricting food. For example, you may want to begin to eat more nuts or homemade, whole-food snacks.

10 Tell your body your commitment to make this change over time to show your body love.

Participate in Joyful Movement

The idea of exercise and working out often feels like serious, heavy work nowadays—you might feel pressured to attend branded classes or join intense outdoor competitions. Ask yourself about the messages you've picked up about exercise. How do these messages affect how you think about movement? Part of taking good care of your body is reclaiming the fun and lightness of inhabiting it. This activity will help you look at exercise and movement as something to look forward to.

Steps:

1 Notice that as a child, your relationship with movement was likely more authentic. Children often move their bodies as a way of having fun and exploring the world. What sorts of movement did you enjoy back then? You may have loved to jump rope, twirl a Hula-Hoop, ride your bike, or climb trees, as examples.

2 How do you feel remembering these activities? Notice your body still craves authentic movement.

3 Pick one activity you loved as a child (you may always pick more later) that you might still like to do. How can you do this again? Perhaps you can dance with a video game or join your kids on the swings at the park.

4 Notice how fun it is just to contemplate movement that you authentically enjoy! Try to commit to practicing this activity once a week.

Speak about Your Body with Respect

Many people's mental chatter is frequently consumed with an inner critic when they have porous boundaries. This inner critic fixates on what's "wrong" in your life or about you. Sadly, this often includes picking apart your body. Protecting your body includes setting limits on how your body is discussed to ensure that it's treated with respect. In an earlier activity, you set limits on the ways others can talk about your body. In this activity, you will set limits as needed on the way *you* speak about your body.

Steps:

1 Start by contemplating how you feel about your body. Do you attack or criticize it? If you are critical toward your body—which most people are until they cultivate boundaries to protect their body—validate why this makes sense. Notice that you have received messages and gone through experiences that impacted your body image. Perhaps you did athletics growing up that stressed a certain body shape, for example.

2 Notice how pervasive messages about the "right" body are in American culture. Also notice that these messages tend to shift and set people up to constantly strive for something new—and feel like their body's not okay.

3 Honor the dialectic: Most people have physical insecurities. These vulnerabilities are a part of being human. At the same time, you can choose to speak to yourself with respect.

4 Commit to setting limits on your inner critic. Think of yourself as acting like a loving parent who tells a verbally abusive person, "No, you may not speak to the child I love in that way."

5 Now pick a specific part of your body that you tend to criticize. Set limits on the inner voice that may start listing multiple things. You can go back and do this exercise again in the future, but for now pick one to be gentle with yourself.

6 Take a breath. What do you appreciate about this part of your body? You may need to think creatively. You might reflect, *My arms allow me to hug the people I love. They also allow me to paint, cook, and do all the necessary tasks of living.* Or you might think, *My thighs allow me to*

stand on my own two feet. Without my thighs, I couldn't walk or dance. My thighs allow me to feel strong in my body. If you keep hearing your critic tell you there's nothing to appreciate, imagine shushing this part as your protective parent self.

7 Imagine sending love to this body part and to your body in general.

8 In the future, when your critic reemerges, reactivate your protective parent mode and set limits on this narrative. Quiet it by restating what you appreciate about your body or this body part in these moments.

Evaluate Your Progress

Healthy boundaries are consistent yet flexible. Earlier in this chapter, you created your sustainable self-care plan in the Make Progress in Five Minutes a Day exercise. Now you will review what's working—or not—about this plan. This assessment allows you to practice consistent yet flexible boundary setting.

Steps:

1 What was the self-care plan you created in the Make Progress in Five Minutes a Day exercise? Have you been able to commit to this plan?

2 If you haven't been able to commit to it, give yourself grace. There are valid barriers to the plan you identified previously. What are the barriers to implementing this change? Example: I wanted to drink more water but despite having my water bottle at work, I keep forgetting to drink out of it because the pace of my work is so hectic. Example: I wanted to go to bed five minutes earlier at night, but my kids' after-school activities keep us out late three nights a week.

3 Validate that you have wonderful intentions *and* your first plan didn't quite yet meet your needs. Based on the barriers you identified, how can you update or change your plan? Practice speaking to yourself like someone you love. For example: I don't drink water in part because I'm not taking my breaks at work. I'm going to start taking my ten-minute morning break. If I choose to drink water at this time, great, but there's no pressure to do this yet. Here's another example: It's not realistic, or kind, to pressure myself to go to bed early nightly. However, we are home on Tuesdays. I will start by going to bed early on Tuesdays. It's okay if it's not the most progress yet—I have to start somewhere.

4 If you have followed through on your plan inconsistently, notice that this too is completely understandable. There are times you won't be able to follow through on your self-care plan for a variety of reasons, including being sick, traveling, or having unexpected events arise. During these times, practice flexibility. Validate that imperfection is human. Example: I've been able to get more sleep most nights—except sometimes I get super into bingeing a TV show. This is okay—I'm focusing on progress, not perfection.

5 If you have been able to commit to this plan, give yourself kudos. It is not easy to set boundaries to protect your health! How do you feel? Do you want to keep this plan as it is? Or do you want to add another activity? You build a self-care lifestyle in which you consistently protect your body, mental health, and relationships step-by-step, like a staircase. Yet you want to add in these changes authentically and in small increments. Here's how that might look: I've been able to stretch nightly before bed. Now, I want to practice deep breathing for a few minutes when I wake up to center myself.

6 No matter how your original plan is going, celebrate yourself for continuing to explore your self-care needs. This is a critical step toward cultivating healthy boundaries.

CHAPTER 7

Protecting Your Money and Your Work

Just like every other aspect of your life, you also need limits around your work and money. Many people understandably struggle to protect these aspects of their life—most of us don't receive clear guidance or support around these topics growing up. Often, what we *are* told is limiting. For example, you may have been told that there are valid and invalid career paths. You may have been discouraged from pursuing your authentic passion for work. Also, many families experience financial insecurity, which can create a lot of fear, uncertainty, and control issues.

The activities in this chapter will help you clearly understand your beliefs, values, and needs around your work and money. You will then cultivate internal limits that can support your views. You will also gain assertive communication skills that can help you champion your right for financial well-being. Finally, you will define exactly what success looks like to you.

Money Impacts Your Sense of Safety

The fundamental goal of boundary setting is to feel safer. Few things impact your sense of safety in this world as noticeably as your relationship with money. This relationship will positively affect your well-being and relationships if you feel secure financially. If you don't, you may experience high levels of stress, which may negatively impact your health and create relationship conflict. Work is addressed in this chapter as well, since work is a primary source of money for many. This chapter addresses unpaid work too, because these contributions often bring up thoughts and feelings around money.

Common boundary issues for work or money include either completely eschewing these types of boundaries or being obsessed with them. The truth is dialectical. Having money matters in the physical world to ensure you feel stable and grounded. But of course, it's not the be-all and end-all—money cannot ever buy you more time and it has only a certain amount of impact on your health. This is precisely why your boundaries around work and money are intrinsically connected to those around your time and health. Without setting boundaries around your time in your pursuits for money and other work, you will miss out on what matters most to you while jeopardizing your health.

Traditional Models of Success Don't Work for Everyone

Your identity and sense of self-worth are commonly tied to your work and finances. It's understandable to gain confidence from your career or accomplishments! But it's important to know that your authentic self is inherently valuable outside of these things. People with porous boundaries around work often fixate on performing and achieving. This makes sense especially because most children are taught a specific model for success: high grades, praise, and scholarships. In adulthood, the traditional model looks like steady jobs, promotions, and raises.

Many people with porous boundaries have worked incredibly hard to achieve what their families or culture told them they "should" become. Yet when they reach the pinnacle of their achievements with the degree, job title, or financial status, they often still feel unhappy and lost. They also often need support processing the pain that arises when they followed the "right" path, but it ended up being wrong for them.

The model of success many of us were taught makes it seem like there are right and wrong paths for your work. It creates the illusion you can follow a specific formula and then be successful. Yet when a person has healthy boundaries, they know that success is tied to their authenticity. No other person can provide the road map for your personal fulfillment. This is why cultivating a connection to your intuition can have many tangible benefits beyond emotional support.

You Are Enough

It's important to set boundaries on the narrative present in various cultures, including American, that your worth comes from your work. In today's busy cultures, people often feel like they're not doing enough. This is a sign of porous boundaries around productivity. The fear of not doing enough highlights that deep down, this person believes *they* are not enough. This idea is reinforced by stories of "self-made" people, which often neglect to mention the support that person got along the way—perhaps in the form of family members' money or connections. These stories can send the toxic message that if you haven't "made it," you just aren't working hard enough. In reality, there are many complex reasons for success, and many versions of authentic success.

Until a person sets boundaries around their work, anxiety and shame often compels them to work harder. Sadly, this is a vicious cycle. You will never find your true self-worth from always working. Rather, you develop greater confidence when you set boundaries on this mentality of "hustle culture." When you honor that all human bodies—yours included—need rest and that it's not a "luxury" or "selfish" to take breaks, you are on your way to having healthy boundaries around work.

Setting these boundaries doesn't make you lazy or greedy. Having time, health, and money are basic rights that you can protect with boundaries. The only people you have the responsibility to provide your money for are dependent children. And even there, it's important to set limits. Many people with porous boundaries around money will live a life of self-neglect, regardless of whether they have money.

Addressing External Money Boundary Violations

Common external boundary violations occur when a person controls your money or withholds it. Having access to money in your relationship is essential for safety and autonomy. If your partner withholds money from you, this is a form of abuse. If you feel safe with your partner communicating your need to have access to money, please do so. If not, you may want to consider attending therapy together to find balance and more safety within your relationship. It's also important to stay safe for others by respecting their right to make choices around how they spend their money—even if you'd make different choices.

Setting and Enforcing Boundaries with Your Workplace

Many people feel scared or intimidated about boundary setting at work. It takes a lot of courage to set boundaries at work, but it's tremendously important. Without boundaries around your work, you will inevitably burn out or face mental or physical health crises. You have the right to set boundaries around your work in order to make the right choices for you and your well-being.

Some corporations unfortunately violate these boundaries by expecting you to ignore your needs, values, time, and health for the sake of the company. A clear sign of this is if you're made out to be the problem if you express your needs or boundaries to the company. You may be told you just need "grit." There may also be pervasive hypocrisy: Your employer may provide lip service to mental health and even give workshops on preventing burnout. Yet, in practice, you may be expected to constantly answer calls—even on your vacation!

Despite these challenges, you *can* influence meaningful change. The more often employees advocate for themselves—during the interview process and throughout their employment—the more empowered employees become. When you have an empowered workforce, they will naturally advocate for balance and wholeness. This collective intention to set boundaries around work has the potential to benefit everyone's well-being, and make the work culture a more joyful place.

Write a Helpful Money Mantra

The human mind tends to seek proof of what it already believes. This phenomenon is called confirmation bias. As such, you naturally look for "proof"—usually unconsciously—of whatever you believe about money. These beliefs about money impact your emotions, actions, and daily life. When these beliefs are supportive, you feel a sense of peace. Unsupportive beliefs about money, however, contribute to anxiety, stress, and issues in relationships. In this activity, you will identify a money belief that is unsupportive and create a new belief that is aligned with your authentic ideal future.

Tools:
Piece of paper and a writing utensil
Sticky note (optional)

Steps:

1 Consider a painful event around money from your life growing up. Just choose one event for now; you can repeat this activity later if needed. Some examples of painful events around money include your family losing their money, inheritance money splitting the family apart, or your family not having enough money for regular meals. Or you may have emotional wounds based on events you didn't personally experience, such as grandparents who grew up during the Great Depression and then may have role-modeled anxiety around money. If you have difficulty identifying any painful experiences, consider what you learned about money growing up. These messages may have been directly expressed or not. Examples include mindsets such as "You must save every penny," "It's greedy to want more than 'just enough' money," or "It's hard to make money." Whatever comes to mind, trust this. Write it at the top of the page.

2 Under that event or message, write down how this experience or message has impacted your relationship with money. For instance, you may save aggressively because of money trauma or spend without limits, believing "Easy come, easy go." Add notes about how this message or event affected your sense of safety and security. What are the long-term consequences of these actions? For example:

- If you believe there is "never enough" money, you may constantly work. You may not be home very often with your kids, and you may neglect self-care. Your long-term health may suffer due to self-neglect. You may later regret you missed out on watching your kids grow up.
- If you believe money is "evil," you may try to reject money. But without money, you may constantly worry how you will pay your bills. Long-term, this stress can be harmful to your health, and you won't have any savings in case of emergencies or as you age. This will create a negative cycle, feeding understandable anxiety.

3   At the bottom of the page, write down what you would like to believe instead. Think about your visual of your future self from the Write the Story of Your Future Self exercise in Chapter 2. To have this life, what must you believe about money? Examples: *I have enough money. Wanting the safety of having money is understandable. When I am passionate about my work, money flows to me. I have the right to earn money and keep some of this for myself.*

4   Write a mantra of this new belief and circle it. For example, you could say "I have more than enough money to care for myself and enjoy my life" or "I can desire money and still be a good person." If desired, write this mantra on a separate piece of paper or sticky note and hang it near your workspace. In the future, if you sense your old belief popping up in your mind, emotions, or actions, set limits on this by stating your new mantra.

Create a Spending Routine Aligned with Your Values

People commonly have an all-or-nothing relationship with money prior to developing healthy boundaries. On one end of the spectrum are people who are afraid of losing all their money so their relationship with it is controlling and restrictive. On the opposite side are people who are so casual in their relationship with money that it feels like grains of sand sliding through their fingers the moment they have it.

In this activity, you will explore an authentic balance in your innate right to choose how you spend your own money.

Steps:

1 Take a moment to contemplate what money represents to you, such as security, freedom, adventure, and fun.

2 Reimagine the bubble from the Visualize Your Boundaries exercise in Chapter 1. Push any fears, insecurities, or others' judgments around money outside of your bubble as necessary.

3 Now consider your top values from the Identify Your Values exercise in Chapter 4. (If you have yet to do this activity, do so now.)

4 With both your values and what money represents to you in mind, brainstorm a list of what it makes sense to spend your money on. There is no right or wrong way to answer this. It is what feels aligned for you. Keep in mind your personal budget as well. (If you feel like you're not making enough money yet, please see the Negotiate a Fair Salary or Raise activity in this chapter.) Here are some examples:
   • I value time with family and money represents freedom. It makes sense to hire a monthly housekeeper to free up my time for family, since I can honestly afford it.
   • Money represents security to me, and I value adventure. I need to pay off debt to feel more secure—and potentially then have more flexibility in the type of work I can do in order to travel more.
   • I value health and money represents fun to me. I'm going to spend some money on a dance class.

5 With your values and your personal meaning of money in mind, now brainstorm where you may want to put limits on your spending. For example:

- I value adventure therefore it makes sense to cut back on my streaming subscriptions because they tempt me to spend my weekends indoors.
- I value authenticity. I will cut back on purchases I make on clothes or tech to feel like I'm "keeping up" with others.

6 Take steps to align your spending habits with your true values in life and around money. You may create a checklist of questions to ask yourself before you buy something online to help. For instance, if you value sustainability, you may want to ask yourself, *Do I already have something I could use for the same purpose?* before you shop online. Or you could use a visual reminder such as putting a tiny sticker that represents a value of yours on your credit card. If you value freedom, maybe a sticker of a bird would help you stay mindful of your desire to pay off debt. You might still experience guilt when you spend authentically. Please know this is completely understandable—and you can simultaneously feel guilty while doing the right thing for you.

Pay Yourself First

There are many possible reasons why people have an imbalanced relationship with money. They may feel obligated or responsible to spend their money on their loved ones or they may be terrified of losing money to the point of living a life of self-denial. In this activity, you will explore the limits you may need to set on yourself to protect your financial—and emotional—well-being and ensure you have a healthy and joyful relationship with money.

Steps:

1 What does the feeling of not having enough money feel like to you? This can be literally not having enough money or a sense that no matter how much money you acquire, it's not "enough." You may notice feelings of stress, overwhelm, anxiety, clinging, desperation, or panic.

2 A healthy relationship with money is balanced. If you are not in the habit of saving any money or spending money on yourself, notice the importance of this.

3 Validate the reasons why you believe saving right now isn't an option. Or if your relationship is more restrictive, validate the reasons why spending money on joy doesn't feel possible. You may also need to validate any money trauma that impacts your sense that you cannot save—or spend—your money. You began to explore this in the first activity in this chapter.

4 If you struggle to keep money for yourself, set limits around this. Open a high-yield savings account. Commit to paying yourself first whenever you acquire money—even if it's just a few dollars in the beginning. This is an essential act of self-care and self-love. Visualize the relief you will feel having money in savings—knowing that even if you find yourself in a bad job or relationship, you have viable options to leave. Having your own money is tremendously empowering.

5 If you struggle to spend money on your joy, think about how money is a tool that allows you to experience the richness of life, which you fully deserve (even if you don't feel this way yet). Identify something joyful to spend your money on. This may be something small at first, such as lunch out weekly. Or if you feel more comfortable you may save for a trip you've always wanted to take. Notice the joy and relief of utilizing the tool of money to experience the richness of life in your limited time here.

Validate Your Earning Potential

People with porous boundaries around their work and their money are underpaid. At times, they may even work for free. This might be because they feel guilty or insecure about charging the appropriate wage for their work. This exercise is designed to boost your confidence by calculating what you have the right to earn.

Tools:
Calculator
Piece of paper and a writing utensil
Electronic device with online access (optional)

Steps:

1 Write down your current hourly wage or yearly salary. Some tips if that number is not readily available:
   - If you don't yet work but are preparing to enter the workforce, search for the average wage for a job at your level in your location and use that number. This applies to creative work as well. If you make handmade cards, for example, explore online shops to see what others are charging.
   - If your contributions in the world are unpaid, such as by being a stay-at-home parent or a volunteer, list the skills necessary for this role, such as cooking, event planning, and accounting. Then go online and search for the average salary for a job in one of these roles.

2 Write down any training or education you completed to prepare for your role. Note how much you invested for this education, both financially and in terms of your time and effort. You can also jot down any informal training you did, such as extensive research on topics to develop or strengthen your skills. Total up how many hours you've spent preparing. Notice that these hours invested validate your right to make at least the average wage—if not more. Remind yourself that your expertise and time are worth respecting, whether you work outside of the home or not. If you violate your own boundaries by doubting your right to charge for your time and expertise, review the wage you determined and hours of preparation as needed to reinforce your confidence.

3 Now identify how many hours you actually work a week. Salaried positions are usually based on forty hours per week, but you may work more than that. If you work time that's not paid, such as by bringing work home, you are diluting your appropriate wage. Example: Let's say you make $28 per hour for a forty-hour-a-week job. Yet you often feel behind so you take work home an extra fifteen hours per week. This means you're only making $20 per hour. What feelings come up when you notice any dilution of your appropriate wage? If you feel righteous anger, this is your sign to set boundaries around your time to protect your money and contributions.

4 Assess what steps to take next. For example:
- If you feel like you can't complete your work in the allotted time you're supposed to work, notice if this is a systemic issue in your company. They may need to hire more people—or at least compensate you for the amount of work given to you.
- If your work is unpaid and you are overextending yourself, this is an opportunity to divide and conquer the workloads. Perhaps you need to communicate with your partner about contributing more at home. If you have children, you may provide them with age-appropriate chores to contribute.

Violations Are Human Nature

Boundary violations happen, in part, because of human nature. People are designed to expend the least amount of energy possible while achieving the maximum reward. Even without intending to, many people—and businesses—will try to take as much as possible from you with as little in return as necessary.

Ask Smart Questions During an Interview

Asking the right questions during a job interview is a good way to assess if a company's culture or the job role will meet your needs and support your boundaries. In this activity, you will identify questions to ask that will help you determine whether a potential employer is a good fit for you.

Steps:

1 Consider your top three ways to feel respected and valued at work. These could include a clear path to promotion, a flexible schedule, or work-life balance. To find joy at work, you must use these as nonnegotiable must-haves.

2 Develop questions to assess if these needs can be met. Here are some examples:
- If you value balance, you might ask, "How do you prevent employee burnout?" or "If an employee is assigned more work than is possible to complete during their scheduled time, how do you approach this situation?"
- If you value flexibility, you could ask, "If I need to change my schedule in the future, how would this be handled?" or "Do I have the opportunity to work from home?"

3 Pay attention to the words the interviewer uses. An employer who expresses a need for "loyalty," "doing whatever is necessary," "going above and beyond," or "being all in" could be sharing signs that they don't offer a balanced, respectful relationship with their employees.

4 Trust your gut. Potential employers can say all the right things yet still feel disingenuous.

Bring Your Dream Life Into Reality

Your vision for your authentic dream life involves money. This is true no matter what you envisioned, given that money is necessary, at least to some degree, in our material world. In this exercise, you will empower yourself to actively create your dream life through your choices around money and work.

Tools:

Piece of paper and a writing utensil, or a digital sketchpad

Steps:

1 Draw a straight horizontal line on your piece of paper—this will represent a timeline. On the right side of your line, describe your authentic dream life. (You might look back at the Write the Story of Your Future Self exercise in Chapter 2.) Create bullet points of all the characteristics of this life, including how you see your home, where you see yourself living, how you dress, the foods you eat, and how and with whom you spend your time.

2 What areas of your dream life include money? What about those that include work? Circle all of these bullet points.

3 When you look at all the things you circled, do all of these things feel aligned to your authentic values? If everything feels aligned in your vision for the future, wonderful. Please move to the next step. If not, please know this is understandable. Sometimes when you begin to consider your dream life, it's initially filled with things you think you "should" want instead of what truly matters most to you. For instance, maybe when you think about it, you notice pursuing a promotion at work prevents you from having more time with your children, which you value highly. If you notice anything that's not aligned, you are cultivating more authentic awareness, which is great. Cross out anything that's not aligned. You can always decide to work toward this later if your values or needs change, but for now allow for the peace of clarifying your vision.

4 Affirm that you may already be taking steps to live into your dream life by writing positive steps you've taken on the far left side of your timeline.

5 Is there anything else on your dream list that you can bring into your life already, even in small ways? Many of us get stuck into automatically and endlessly thinking that it's "not the right time" for the life we really want. This understandable but unhelpful thought keeps many of us waiting indefinitely to truly live authentically. Write down any small steps you can take next, noting them on the timeline to the right of the steps you're already taking. Here's an example: On the left side of your page you affirm that you have begun to take your days off rather than giving up this time you earned. You may not yet be able to afford to only work four days a week; however, you can use PTO for a day off each month. Then you may notice that to get down to four workdays a week, you'll first need to pay off your credit card debt. Note this as another mark on your timeline as a future goal to get you to your eventual four-day-workweek goal, which appears on the right side of the line.

6 Commit to taking one small action step to live closer into your dream life. If there's anything you need to schedule, e.g., PTO or a massage, please do so to complete this exercise. Affirm yourself—this is important work! Every step you take in the direction of your authentic dream life brings it closer to your reality.

Negotiate a Fair Salary or Raise

Many people with porous boundaries have experienced the pain of learning they make less than others in the same role because they didn't assert themselves to ask for a fair salary when taking a new job. If you provide a service, honor your fair wage—even with friends. It's a boundary violation to be expected to work for free or less than what makes you feel respected. If you're looking for a job, allow this respectful wage to be nonnegotiable. Otherwise, you will feel resentful later. This activity will provide you with the opportunity to practice assertive communication around financial negotiations.

Steps:

1 First, determine what wage or salary will make you feel respected in your work (or on a project). Notice the difference you feel emotionally between considering what would make you feel respected versus what you're currently being paid.

2 When discussing pay **during the interview process**, say something like, "I appreciate that offer, but I need to get closer to [larger number than nonnegotiable]." You must advocate for yourself to counteract the human nature that company representatives will show (they will take as much as they can get for as little as possible). Employers expect to negotiate, so state a number higher than your ideal wage. If an employer rejects you, they revealed they aren't a good choice for you as you're starting this relationship from a place of too much self-sacrifice.

3 If you're already in a job, it's essential to **advocate for a raise**. You may have understandable fears or guilt, but you're the only person who can protect your financial well-being. Use this outline for assistance:
   • Say or email, "I need to have my yearly evaluation by [give a date within the month]."
   • Before the meeting, if possible, find out the yearly cap for raises (this may be in the employee handbook).
   • During this meeting, note the length of time you have worked there and any accomplishments. For example, if you have been doing the job of others as they eliminated roles, discuss this. State, "Based on this increased work (or accomplishments), I need to get a raise."

I'm hoping for [state maximum they offer yearly]." Now you can negotiate.

- If your request for an evaluation and/or raise is rejected, no matter the justifications, your boundaries are being violated. Your financial boundaries are violated when you are not given career advancement opportunities, including raises, or if barriers are put in place, such as penalizing you for taking maternity leave. This employer has revealed they don't value an interdependent, safe relationship together. Prioritize your well-being over the employer's. Update your resume and look for a more respectful company. This may feel like a lot of work at first, but notice the future relief of being valued—and earning more money.

A Raise or a New Job?

Many employers justify not giving raises, so be sure to explore your other options. The Pew Research Center found in 2022 that people who stayed with their current employers from April 2021 to March 2022 saw their "real" wage (after adjusting for inflation) drop by 1.7 percent for the median worker. But half of those who switched employers had their real wage increase by at least 9.7 percent!

Create Your Authentic Definition of Success

It's easy to tie your identity to your career or financial status in a culture that stresses wealth and productivity. But this is a very fragile, vulnerable way to live. After all, if your work or money is compromised, you will then have an identity crisis. To protect yourself, it's important to explore your authentic definition of success. You'll do just that in this activity.

Tools:
Piece of paper and a writing utensil

Steps:

1 Divide your paper into three columns. In the first one, jot down what you learned that you "should" want as you were growing up. What did you learn about success? Did you learn that certain careers or paths were valid, and others weren't? How did these messages affect your relationship to your passions?

2 In the second column, reflect on how these messages impacted your career path. Perhaps you worked very hard to achieve the job you "should" have but now you feel empty. Did these messages impact your finances? If you learned that what you do isn't a "real job," you may struggle to charge the wage you deserve. Does your chosen career path impact your self-worth?

3 In the third column, try to write a more authentic definition of success that's based on your values, not necessarily what you heard growing up. While your work and money are a part of your life, you are more than these things too. To feel happy—and successful—it's important to live in alignment with your authentic values. What is *your* version of success? For instance, your authentic definition might include your work along with things like healing from trauma, being a good parent, or learning how to be happy.

Communicate with Your Partner about Money

Money is a frequent source of conflict for many couples. Commonly, this occurs because each person has different goals for spending and saving, or different experiences and values around money. If you add in unclear communication on the topic on top of those differences, it's easy to see how a conflict develops.

In this activity, you will develop communication skills that will help you and your partner share needs around money in a clearer way. This allows for greater intimacy and understanding while compromising as needed to both live into your desired future.

Steps:

1 Take time to ask your partner, "What does money represent to you?" If your partner is unsure, you may support them by offering examples. People commonly view money as a source of freedom, safety, or fun.

2 Once your partner shares, communicate what money represents to you. Your partner's view of money is likely different from yours. Very rarely does this perfectly align, which is why money often leads to arguments. Understand that these differences are natural and they can be successfully worked through.

3 Ask your partner, "What are your biggest goals or needs around money?" Allow yourself to remain curious and open-minded. Again, it's completely okay if their answer is different from yours. (If you aren't partnered but live with your parents, for example, you may need clarity on their expectations for you paying rent or when you will move out.)

4 Validate that these goals make sense. Then share your own. Even if you don't make your own money, it's still important to advocate for your long-term well-being in the case of illness, death, or divorce.

5 If your needs or goals match, discuss your plan to meet these goals together. Be sure to review needs and boundaries in your relationship from time to time, even if you tend to agree.

6 If your goals are different, remember healthy boundaries are flexible. It's important to compromise where you can. You also have the responsibility

to be safe for others, which means you don't have the right to control or dictate your partner's spending. Rather, you can negotiate together:

- First, set limits on any guilt or obligation you may feel about meeting your partner's needs above your own.
- Identify ways to meet each goal through compromise and planning. For example, if you want to pay off debt while your partner wants to go on an international vacation, explore ways to meet in the middle. Perhaps you may agree that your primary paychecks can go toward credit card debt. As a bonus, you may ensure that you're using cards that provide you with rewards for travel. Then you may agree that any extra money earned, like with a side gig, can go toward saving for a vacation.

What Is Financial Infidelity?

Financial infidelity is when one partner lies about purchases or hides income or debt. When this happens, feelings of trust and safety are often destroyed in the relationship. Rebuilding trust is a complex process. If you're struggling to rebuild trust, ask for the support of a couples therapist.

Prevent (or Manage) Burnout from Working Too Hard

Are you burnt-out? Many people, especially those in their forties, report hitting a wall. They can't function on the superhuman level they've become accustomed to, and sometimes they can't even find the energy to get out of bed or brush their teeth. Do you ever feel this drained?

American culture tends to overlook the prevention of mental or physical health issues for the sake of productivity. The prevailing opinion is that it's understandable to take time off if you get sick with something serious, like cancer, but taking time to rest to prevent illness is "lazy" or "self-indulgent." Sadly, this attitude reinforces porous boundaries around time and work, which then leads to burnout and illness. In this activity, you will prevent (or manage) burnout.

Steps:

1 Recognize any messages you are holding on to that negatively judge taking time off. Set limits on internal fears like being "lazy" if you take time for rest. You may also need to set limits on finding self-worth in how much you work or how little you sleep. You can revisit the Set Internal Limits to Be Safe with Yourself exercise in Chapter 1 to remind yourself of this process.

2 If possible, schedule time off from work.
   - If you find yourself immediately saying you can't do that, push back on reasons why this isn't possible. For encouragement, consider that research shows employees who take less than ten days off a year have a 34.6 percent chance of getting a raise or promotion, but those who take more than ten days off are 65.4 percent likely to get a raise or promotion!
   - If your contributions are unpaid, such as being a stay-at-home parent, consider taking regularly scheduled time for yourself. It may be hard to overcome reasons why this isn't possible, but please know that if you burn out, you won't be available to your family for much longer periods if you need time to recover.

3 If you're getting less than seven hours of sleep regularly, prioritize your need for sleep. Research shows there are many negative consequences from a lack of sleep, such as a greater risk of obesity, depression, memory

issues, impaired decision making, increased conflict in relationships, and even heart failure. You may, for instance, set a timer when you watch TV at night to ensure you go to bed twenty minutes earlier now. Consistent self-care allows you to show up for your loved ones and your work as your best self. But to remain consistent changes must be made in sustainable small steps.

4   You're being courageous setting limits on hustle culture! Affirm yourself as needed with these affirmations (or any other you want): "It's a basic human need to rest and sleep. I show up for what I value better when I'm well rested. I have the right to not work in this moment. I have the right to rest and sleep."

Protecting Your Relationships

Learning how to effectively yet kindly set boundaries with others is many people's primary reason for starting a boundary-setting journey. You have laid the foundation in Parts 1 and 2 to now protect your relationships with others. You will take what you have learned about your authentic needs, wants, and limits to express yourself clearly and honestly with others while respecting them.

Balance is the primary focus of Part 3. Here, you will cultivate interdependent relationships that have healthy boundaries alongside closeness and support. This is the opposite of relationships where you may get preoccupied by another person's feelings or needs, which is sometimes called codependency. It's also the opposite of being overly independent as this prevents genuine intimacy. Here you will balance a sense of trust and safety while being appropriately vulnerable.

This part starts with your family, as these relationships are often the most emotional to set boundaries within. Because guilt trips are a common boundary violation within families, two separate activities examine these. You will then focus on boundaries in intimate relationships, which includes ensuring your sexual limits are respected. Finally, you will set boundaries to protect your friendships and relationships in general to allow yourself to be authentic with others in a way that feels safe. In each of these chapters, you will be invited to use assertive communication skills. For review and practice refer back to the Assert Your Limits exercise in Chapter 1.

CHAPTER 8

Protecting Your Relationships with Family

Many people enter adulthood with clear emotional wounds from their childhood due to their family not understanding or respecting boundaries. If that's the case, know that you are incredibly brave to make a different choice now. If you have clear childhood trauma from within your family, please take breaks throughout this chapter as you need, and consider getting extra support from a therapist. When you are exploring your current mindset and how you acquired it, things naturally feel a little worse before they get better. Seeking extra support, if you feel called to it, is courageous and wise.

Even if you feel you've had a good childhood, this chapter may stir up complex emotions or painful memories. It's common to discover violations that did occur in your family as you learn more about healthy boundaries. If this happens, please take your time and be gentle with yourself. No matter your personal history, this chapter will help you explore how to nurture positive relationships with family members while protecting your authentic relationship with yourself.

Looking Back Gives You Clarity

For many people, setting boundaries with family is the most confusing, complex, and intimidating work in the entire journey. While all humans have the basic need for belonging, this need typically and most profoundly presents itself within a family. It's a primal urge to want to feel seen, respected, and understood by your family.

You may have had the experience of having a close, loving family growing up, which continues today. If so, this is a gift to celebrate. You may still over the course of this process discover some wounds around your boundaries in your family. This is completely natural. Keep in mind that the goal of exploring your childhood is not to judge or criticize your parents, caregivers, or any other family members. The vast majority of parents are doing their absolute best with the tools they were provided by their own families growing up.

The goal of exploring your childhood—whether in therapy or in a book like this—is to help you connect the dots and gain important insight into your own beliefs and behaviors. Your experiences with your caregivers laid the foundation for how you currently understand your feelings, needs, desires, and limits. These experiences also are the basis for your relationship with yourself and your acceptance, or rejection, of your authenticity. Sadly, for many of us our first wounds to our authentic self and sense of worth occurred within our families growing up. This may have been completely unintentional, and yet you may still have picked up messages that your authentic needs, feelings, or limits were not acceptable growing up.

Remember Dialectical Thinking

Dialectical thinking remains important as you explore your history with your family. You may have been nurtured and supported in some ways *and* limited in other ways. You can honor, appreciate, and celebrate the aspects of your family that empower you *and* simultaneously honor any experiences that left you feeling disempowered, even if this was completely unintentional. When you honor the disempowering parts, you are able to build more self-compassion as to why it's completely understandable you may struggle with boundaries at times.

Overcoming Enmeshment

One of your most basic rights in your family—and in any other relationship— is to be a whole, authentic person. Yet narratives of obligation and feelings of guilt commonly arise in family relationships. You may have learned that it's more important to be who others want you to be rather than being authentic.

You must reclaim your own voice rather than giving in to the idea that honesty is cruelty or that silence is love.

All relationships deserve boundaries, even if you are very physically and emotionally close to someone. Trying to exist within other people's boundaries is called enmeshment, and it is a common boundary violation in relationships or families. One of the painful consequences of enmeshment is picking up a message that you don't have the right to boundaries. Boundaries may have been labeled as mean or simply unnecessary. A clear sign you experienced enmeshment is if you felt smothered by a parent growing up.

You have the right to privacy, but in enmeshed families, this inherent right is often violated. You might have felt obligated to share everything with a parent who was also your best friend, for instance. Or this boundary would have been violated if someone in your family read your diary or text messages. This experience often feels traumatic because it sends the message you don't have privacy—or safety—anywhere. People with such violations often feel confused as to who is the expert of their experience—themselves or their family member.

Enmeshment hinders emotional development and healthy relationship skills because instead of being guided toward being an individual as you grew up, you may feel responsible for doing what your parent wants or making them happy. Yet you are also a separate person. You are not your parent's therapist or their parent. It's not your fault—or your responsibility—if your parents haven't done their healing work. It's also not your job to protect your parents from the natural consequences of their choices—in other words, your need for greater self-protection now.

When a person has experienced enmeshment and/or other wounding in their family, it may feel like their boundaries have to be all or nothing. It may seem like you have to be either enmeshed or estranged. But there is an ideal state where you evolve into your own authentically separate person. You can figure out how close or distant you need to be from family to feel truly safe. The activities here will provide an overview of these important concepts, and offer some ways to implement boundaries in safe and healthy ways.

Identify Your Family Role

Ideally, as a child develops, they have the space and freedom to discover their authentic self. This process greatly supports healthy boundary-setting skills. For many kids, however, this process doesn't happen fully or at all. In those cases, children often take on a specific role within the family that can be based on their family's expectations, messages they've received, or cultural narratives. In this activity, you will explore whether you have been assigned a family role or roles. If so, you will set boundaries with your family role(s) to be sure you are living your most authentic life.

Tools:
Writing utensil

Steps:

1 Review these common roles and circle any that apply to you:
- ❑ Growing up, did you feel like you had to be perfect? Maybe you needed to look a certain way, get good grades, or perform athletically. If so, you may have been assigned the role of the **Hero.**
- ❑ Do you feel like you are betraying your parents or family if you notice the problems within it? You may be the **Hero**, the **Enabler**, or the **Mascot** if so.
- ❑ Growing up, did you feel like you had to take care of one, or both, parents or your siblings? If so, you're likely in the role of the **Enabler** and/or **Hero.**
- ❑ Did you feel like you had to be funny to diffuse the stress in your family? If so, you may have been assigned the **Mascot** role.
- ❑ When you were a child, did you feel ignored? Maybe you had a sibling with a chronic illness and you felt unseen? Did you feel like no matter how hard you tried, you would never be seen as attractive, funny, smart, deserving, etc. as your sibling? If so, you are likely in the **Lost Child** role.
- ❑ Did you feel like all of the problems in your family were blamed on you? Did you feel like no matter what, you seemed to always be in trouble? If so, you may be the family **Scapegoat.**

2 Take a moment to validate that if you were assigned one or more roles, this has naturally impacted your relationship with your true self.

3 Ask yourself what's not authentic in your life because you're trying to please your family as your assigned role. For example, an Enabler may resent having to be the one who helps a family member out after that family member chose to neglect their health for years.

4 Now consider whether you may make inauthentic choices in an effort to rebel against your role. For example, if you were the Scapegoat, you may have become a nurse to show how kind you are. Or if you were the Hero, you may now abuse drugs to show you can be wild.

5 Brainstorm a small step you can take to set limits on this childhood role and be your true self with your family. Maybe if you always dress perfectly as the Hero, you could wear casual clothes for dinner. Or if you were a Lost Child, you could share a differing viewpoint on a TV show to exercise your voice.

Determine Safe and Unsafe Topics

You don't need to agree on every topic to have a healthy relationship with others. In fact, you probably *won't* agree on every topic, as you are separate people with your own authentic views. True intimacy comes from learning how to respect others' beliefs while validating your right to your own views. Learning how to agree to disagree is one of the kindest and most loving thing you can do for the other person and yourself. This activity will show you how.

Steps:

1 Can you identify any family members with whom you sometimes have stressful interactions due to your differing beliefs? These differences could be about politics, what sort of education or career you should have, or about certain lifestyle choices, like getting married or having kids.

2 Are there specific topics about which you feel a strong urge to debate, argue, or justify yourself? These are topics that are best to avoid with family members (or others).

3 If this topic comes up in the future, set a boundary. First, internally validate your own views. You don't need to debate or judge your own viewpoints. Then let the person know that you don't want to discuss this topic. You can practice this in various ways if you don't yet feel ready to assert yourself, including role-playing this with a friend, writing these statements in your journal, or saying these things in front of a mirror. Practice asserting your limit until you feel more empowered with one of these methods:

- Clearly assert, "I find this topic stressful given our differences. I'm hoping we can change the subject."
- Remove yourself from the situation. You could excuse yourself to go to the restroom or help clean up, for instance.
- Gently change the topic by making a kind joke such as, "It seems best we avoid this topic as we may bore others with our debate."
- If you feel pressured to make certain choices such as have kids or get married, you can let your family member(s) know, "I would prefer not to discuss this anymore until I have an update, which I'll be sure to share if I do. Thank you for respecting this."

Develop Authentic Holiday Celebrations

Navigating the holidays with family is a common source of stress, obligation, and guilt. Or, if you aren't close to your family, the holidays understandably can bring up feelings of pain, loneliness, grief, and even traumatic memories. Whatever your experience of the holidays, you have the right to celebrate the holidays authentically. In this activity, you will take a moment to decide how you want to spend holidays.

Tools:
Piece of paper and a writing utensil

Steps:

1 What is your anchor word from the Build Hope with an Anchor Word exercise in Chapter 2? Does this fit how you want to feel over the holidays? If not, what word represents your authentic desire for holiday celebrations? Write your chosen word in a large heart in the middle of the page.

2 To live in alignment with your authentic vision for the holidays, what behavior or tradition do you need to release? If you want connection, you may need to stop planning weeks of activities to make the holidays "perfect" for your children. If you want relaxation, you may need to limit how many gifts you purchase or choose not to travel. Write these things in the space outside the heart.

3 What is one thing you would like to say yes to for holiday celebrations? If you want connection, you may plan one or two activities for the holidays to be mindfully present with your family rather than being stressed. Write these inside the heart.

4 Try to implement your suggestions. Feel free to pick a small goal to start—you can always do more later.

Reconcile Unhelpful Childhood Messages about Your Emotions

Your emotions provide insight into your boundaries, but many people didn't get clear guidance on their emotions as children. They may even have been told by loved ones that their emotions were wrong or invalid. If you didn't get guidance around emotions and/or were shamed for them, you may struggle to cope in healthy ways. You may act like your parents did in response to their emotions or cope in the complete opposite way you witnessed. This activity will support you in developing or deepening a balanced, healthy relationship with your emotions based on your current needs, not your childhood norms. First, you'll explore the messages you received about your emotions; then you'll consider the coping mechanisms that were modeled for you.

Steps:

1 Let's first examine your childhood experiences around emotions. What messages did you receive growing up about your emotions? For example, you may have heard that you were "too sensitive" or "needy." When you expressed your concerns or wounds, were you told you were being dramatic or acting like a victim? If so, notice this truth with compassion for your family members who treated you like that and also compassion for yourself. They may not have been trying to hurt you and yet still impacted your relationship with your emotions.

2 How have these messages impacted the way you feel and/or cope with your emotions now? For example, maybe you shove your emotions down or refuse to cry. Or perhaps you see yourself as weak because you tend to feel deeply. You might also attack yourself with the same words that your parents used in reaction to your emotions.

3 Visualize pushing these old beliefs out of your bubble (from the Visualize Your Boundaries exercise in Chapter 1) as necessary. Think about limits you may want to set around these messages you picked up. The next time someone criticizes your sensitivity, for example, you could share that you think there's value in deep feelings.

4 What do you authentically believe about your emotions? What would your future self (from the Write the Story of Your Future Self exercise in Chapter 2) say to you about the gift of your emotions?

5 If you'd like, create an affirmation to honor your authentic belief around your emotions. To reclaim your sensitivity, for example, you could say, "My sensitivity is a gift. It allows me to feel deeply and connect with others. It helps me be self-aware."

6 Now let's move on to coping strategies. How did your caregivers and other important people in your life cope with their emotions when you were growing up? Did you have role models for healthy coping strategies or did family members struggle to care for their mental well-being? If you witnessed unhealthy coping strategies, do you emulate these behaviors when you are distressed? Or do you act in the opposite way for any of these behaviors? For example, if your dad would drink and give the silent treatment when he was upset, while your mom would yell, you might have made a choice to act more like your dad than your mom by avoiding people if they upset you rather than yelling at them. You might tell people "I'm too busy to talk" if you're angry.

7 How do you authentically want to care for your emotions today? If you already completed Chapter 5, build off this work. You may want to allow yourself space to rest, get into nature, or journal.

Stand Up for Yourself (Even with People You Love)

Setting boundaries necessitates owning your right to use your voice. Yet this may be especially hard if, as it commonly happens, your first experiences with being silenced were within your family. In this activity, you'll explore how you may have been silenced and learn how to assert yourself with more confidence moving forward.

Steps:

1 Did you ever feel silenced growing up? If so, what made you believe that your authentic voice was "too much" or "not good enough"? Did you pick up any messages in your family that complicate your ability to assert yourself? These could have been messages such as "Children should be seen, not heard" or "You can't be angry; you must forgive and forget."

2 Do you still silence yourself at times as an adult? Maybe you minimize your concerns by saying that whatever bothers you isn't "that bad." Or you might gaslight yourself by saying things like "nothing really awful happened" to silence yourself.

3 When you think about being silenced by yourself or others, what image comes to mind? Let your intuition guide you.

4 Now imagine yourself feeling empowered enough to use your voice, as you need, to protect yourself. What image comes to mind now?

5 When you need to assert yourself moving forward, visualize embodying your empowered image. Remain courageous even though the task is challenging.

Manage Guilt Trips

Guilt trips are a common reason you may sometimes ignore your needs and limits with your family. Whatever your family members' intentions, when they are guilt-tripping you, they are trying to manipulate you to prioritize their needs over yours. This is often not intentional but is not loving or respectful all the same. Guilt trips by family members or others are a violation of your time. Remember your boundary bubble from the Visualize Your Boundaries exercise in Chapter 1: You decide what comes in and what stays out. Make sure your need or limit is firm, otherwise you are giving the guilt tripper permission to violate your boundary. This will cause later stress, frustration, and resentment. This exercise will give you tips on how to deal with these tricky situations.

Steps:

1 Use the script from the Assert Your Limits exercise in Chapter 1 to assert yourself with a family member who guilt-trips you. Anticipate you may need to take the following additional steps.

2 Notice your feelings once you express your boundary or need. Do you feel respected? Great, you had a successful interaction around your boundaries with this family member! If you feel internal conflict— perhaps a sense of guilt or obligation alongside feelings of frustration or like you're being misunderstood—continue on.

3 Remember, this situation is dialectical. It's possible for someone to love you *and* you may still need to protect yourself from them sometimes.

4 Validate that you may feel guilty and yet this is likely false guilt. You feel false guilt when you go against what you've learned you "should" do. Authentic guilt happens when you violate your own values. You aren't doing anything wrong by asserting your separate needs to your family member.

5 Use the following script for support when you are being guilt-tripped. You can still be kind and validating, but must reiterate your need:
   • "I understand that [validate their objection to your boundary]."
   • "Yet I need [reiterate your boundary—you may provide a brief reason of no more than a few sentences]."

- Optional: "Please know [validate their objection with your own feelings if a part of you shares the feelings they expressed]."
- "I really appreciate your understanding that I need [restate your limit]."
- Express your love for them briefly if you'd like, but be careful to not "fix" the situation by giving inauthentic promises. Here's an example:

    "I understand you want me to come home for Thanksgiving. Yet I need to stay home this year because I just switched jobs. I don't have any time off yet, and I'm not up to all that traveling over three days. Please know I'll miss you too on Thanksgiving. I really appreciate your understanding that I need to stay home this year." (Note: I didn't say I'll be home for Christmas because I'm not yet sure this is possible.)

6 If you experience pushback, take a break from the conversation. It's not healthy for either of you to debate your valid needs.

You're Not Obligated to Soothe Others

People use guilt trips when they choose to not soothe themselves when they don't get what they want. They instead look to you then to be their source of comfort. While it's your responsibility to assert yourself, it's not your job to soothe them. It's the other person's responsibility to learn how to self-soothe.

Stop Guilt-Tripping Yourself

Do you ever avoid setting boundaries because you feel obligated to return all you "owe" to your parents or other family members? Or you may be afraid of "ruining" the relationship by setting limits. This is a way of guilt-tripping yourself. If you guilt yourself, you may also inadvertently gaslight yourself to avoid facing a difficult part of your childhood. You may tell yourself that what you experienced wasn't *that* bad or that you're misinterpreting a situation. You may also justify why it's okay that your family member violates your limits.

You can have compassion for your family members while honoring your right to your authenticity. You have the right to your own separate needs and desires from everyone else including your family members and loved ones. When you deny this right, you deny your very right to be human. In this activity, you will explore how to interrupt a self-guilting narrative and prioritize your needs.

Tools:
Piece of paper and a writing utensil

Steps:

1 Think about a situation in which you may need to set boundaries, but you keep second-guessing it or procrastinating. Write down the situation and why you may have been delaying. Think about the beliefs you picked up that may reinforce your guilt and prevent your boundary setting.
   - If you feel you must parent your parent(s), you will likely feel responsible to keep them comfortable.
   - If you were guilted a lot by family, you may use this same language to guilt yourself. For example, you may tell yourself that even if you're exhausted, you need to go see your dad because he's already eighty-six years old and you may be giving up your last time to see him before he dies.

2 Has there ever been a time you didn't set a boundary because of guilt? Were there negative consequences because of this avoidance? Jot down what happened. Ultimately, hiding your needs harms your relationships with yourself and others.

- Maybe you didn't want to be mad at your mother-in-law because she "does so much for you" (like helping with childcare) so you shoved your feelings down. Then maybe you found yourself snapping at her for something trivial.
- If you have felt responsible to be your parent's source of comfort, you may feel constantly drained and like you have lost yourself.

3 Consider if you may be able to change your relationship with guilt. Here are some ideas:

- **Adjust your mindset.** Maybe you can begin to see feeling guilty as a sign that you are truly making progress in your boundary setting and being courageous.
- **Cope well with your guilt.** Practice self-soothing—review Chapter 5 for guidance. Instead of stewing in guilt, try to transform it by doing something loving and fun just for you like listening to a song you love or using that bath bomb or anything else you've been waiting to use for a "special occasion."
- **Choose to honor yourself even in the face of the guilt.** Set the boundaries you need even if you feel guilty. Remember, a healthy parent doesn't pressure their child to do something that hurts them.

4 You may not yet feel ready to eliminate guilt altogether, and that's okay. This will come with lots of practice.

Accept Complex Feelings Toward Your Family

As humans, our thinking naturally—but mistakenly—skews to wanting to categorize things as "good" or "bad"…like our feelings. Yet it's completely natural to have complex and even contradictory emotions. Have you noticed this toward your family or any specific family members?

Learning to identify and accept your emotions is an essential part of effective boundary setting. Your emotions, even when they're uncomfortable, provide you valuable insights into your needs, wants, and limits when you accept them. Plus, acknowledging your emotions dialectically can help. This type of thinking highlights that one or more things that seem like opposites can be true. You may be jealous of your sister yet admire her. You may resent your father for being gone a lot for work while you were growing up, yet appreciate all he's provided. If you ignore your feelings or tell yourself not to feel that way, you miss out on taking the clearest path toward setting boundaries. In this activity, you will practice accepting your complex emotions related to your family.

Tools:
Piece of paper and a writing utensil

Steps:

1 What are some of your complex or contradictory emotions you feel toward family? Write these down in a list on the page. It's completely acceptable to have many emotions toward certain family members. Example: *I love my mom more than anyone, yet I also sometimes feel I hate her if I'm being honest. She frustrates me and I feel misunderstood. But I also admire her.*

2 Which of these emotions are rooted in the present day? Circle these.

3 Which emotions are more rooted in the past or in what happened in your childhood? Underline these. Your past emotions are completely understandable and valid. These are likely related to wounding experiences with this family member, even if it was completely unintentional on their part. Family roles could also contribute to these emotions you're carrying from the past. The feelings you underlined may also be signs you still don't feel completely safe in this relationship.

It's important to understand your needs for safety. (The next activity will help you assess this.)

4 Any current uncomfortable emotions highlight areas where you need to set boundaries. What are your feelings revealing? For example, you might think, *I'm frustrated my mom calls me all day when I'm at work. I need her to respect I'm not available during the workday.*

The Power of Letting Go

The emotions you're carrying from the past can weigh you down. In therapy, it's often said that depression is reinforced by a focus on the past. While your feelings are valid, it's important to learn how to let go of the past for your own well-being. This is multilayered therapeutic work that starts after someone has begun to set boundaries.

Determine What Level of Connection
Is Safe or Right for You

When processing family issues, a common question that comes up is whether you need to cut family members out entirely, or just accept them as they are. Of course, there is no one right answer—everyone's situations and needs are different. The key is assessing your options and spending some time figuring out the right answer *for you*. This activity will help you do that.

Steps:

1 Identify a family member with whom you have conflict and consider what option is right for your situation:

- **Stay enmeshed** and let them do, or say, whatever they want by not setting limits. The benefit of staying enmeshed is you can maintain the relationship exactly as is—you don't need to do anything new. However, the risk is you will likely continue to expose yourself to behaviors and comments that are painful for you. Another risk of staying enmeshed is feeling guilty or ashamed for having different thoughts or needs from the other person. This naturally complicates all of your boundary-setting work.

- **Assert your limits** (see the Assert Your Limits exercise in Chapter 1). The benefit of asserting yourself is you are empowered to influence change in your relationship. If the other person is receptive, you can improve the dynamics within the relationship that are stressful or upsetting. On the other hand, even if they're not receptive, you begin to build the confidence that comes from using your voice. The risk of asserting yourself is that the other person may not be willing to respect your needs. This may make you feel like it was "pointless" to assert yourself, but there is value in empowering yourself to see how safe—or unsafe—a person is for you.

- **Stay in their life but create distance.** You could still see them, but less often, for example. The benefit of this is you do not have to assert yourself, which can be very intimidating. Additionally, this may be the best option if you already know that this person is highly defensive when they're spoken to regarding their behaviors. The risk is that you may feel you are betraying yourself by not speaking up or by keeping this person in your life.

- **Cut off contact.** You always have this right. Feeling safe—and being safe for others—are the primary goals of boundary setting. If you're struggling to forgive your family member and find you're unkind at times because of this, sometimes the most loving thing you can do for now, for both of you, is take space apart from them. If it seems drastic, remember that you can take space as needed now, and explore bringing this person back into your life later; healthy boundaries are flexible and your needs may evolve over time.

2 **Important note:** If you're experiencing active abuse, tap into your self-protection skills. You could imagine yourself as a mama bear saying "enough" to protect her cub. Would you want your child, or any child for that matter, to accept being treated the way you are being treated? If not, at the very least, keep setting boundaries, and strongly consider more drastic measures.

CHAPTER 9

Protecting Your Intimate Relationships

There is no perfect relationship—regardless of what you see on social media—but there are safe and unsafe relationships. Healthy, safe relationships are free from abuse, whether it's emotional, financial, verbal, physical, and/or sexual in nature. How your partner (or anyone else) responds to your boundary setting is what's most revealing about whether a relationship is safe and healthy or not. This concept will be explored throughout this chapter and its activities.

Even in healthy relationships, boundary setting can make the relationship temporarily feel worse. When boundaries are set, the status quo is challenged, which is not easy to navigate. But when two people feel safe in a relationship, they can discover how to navigate the bumps in the road and, ultimately, feel more connected while doing so.

The activities in this chapter will teach you skills commonly taught in individual and couples therapy. If you're not in a romantic partnership, this chapter is still highly useful for learning to set boundaries in close relationships—just modify the language as you need.

What's Your Attachment Style?

In intimate relationships, your attachment style often reveals the current state of your boundaries. Attachment theory asserts that human beings have the primal need for closeness and intimacy with other people. If your experiences growing up and throughout adulthood have shown you that you can consistently rely on others in a way that feels safe for you, you develop the most balanced attachment style—secure. This attachment style naturally lends itself to having interdependent relationships, which are partnerships in which you trust that your feelings, boundaries, and desires matter to the other person and you care about their feelings, boundaries, and desires as well.

In therapy, a common sign someone has porous boundaries in their intimate relationships is if they spend the majority of their session discussing and analyzing their partner's perspective, needs, and wants. While this focus on their partner comes from a loving place, it also tends to stem from a place of insecurity. Porous boundaries like this often indicate anxious attachment. People with anxious attachment often feel afraid of being abandoned, and therefore they work hard to please others to ensure their belonging in a relationship or group. These wounds may have occurred in childhood either in their family or with peers, including trauma from bullying or moving so often they didn't form close relationships. These wounds could also have occurred in adulthood, such as by being cheated on by a trusted partner.

Other people have walled-off boundaries, and this is called avoidant attachment. These people often create a lot of distractions outside of the relationship, such as through a preoccupation with work, to avoid intimacy. Finally, some people have a combination of these presentations of boundaries, which is called anxious-avoidant attachment style.

While it may seem logical that it's harder to get close to a person with avoidant attachment because of their walled-off boundaries, it's also difficult to be intimate with people with anxious attachment. True intimacy requires that you show up wholly and authentically to be known by your partner, and vice versa. When you neglect your own needs, wants, and boundaries to keep someone else happy, you don't allow your partner the opportunity to truly know you. You can make changes to your attachment style, but not by focusing on the other person—or avoiding them. Instead, cultivating healthy, balanced relationships through boundary setting provides you the opportunity to develop secure attachment.

Recognizing Abuse

People are often confused as to what's healthy or unhealthy in relationships. While for most people, physical abuse is clear, many people struggle to identify emotional abuse. This is completely understandable if you didn't have healthy relationship role models growing up, which many people didn't. Furthermore, American culture as a whole sometimes conflates problematic abusive behaviors with a "whirlwind" romance or other positive-seeming associations.

When you set boundaries, you discover how safe and healthy or unsafe a person may be for you. If your partner (or anyone else) responds in a validating way and works to respect your limits—even if they've been hurtful in the past—this is a hopeful sign. If, on the other hand, you are met with anger, blame, or the silent treatment when you set limits, this is concerning. In such relationships, get the extra support of a couples therapist to make these relationships healthier.

In unhealthy cultures and relationships, the person trying to set boundaries is often scapegoated—meaning, they are turned into the problem. They will often be told they're too sensitive, which is a form of gaslighting. Gaslighting is a highly confusing form of emotional abuse. Gaslighting acts to manipulate your reality (for extra support on how to respond to this, see Chapter 3). A clear sign of gaslighting is if you believe you're the problem in the relationship or if you feel "crazy" because your partner says things you know to be untrue. If your partner is gaslighting, they will reinforce this narrative by throwing your concerns back in your face consistently. A common example of this is a person who tells you that *you're* the reason they did or said the hurtful or offensive thing they did. These people will say that they only yelled at you because you never listen. Or they will repeatedly ask, "What about me?" whenever you share a concern. Relationship problems—unless they occur in a highly abusive environment—are co-created. You are never the sole problem for relationship issues, no matter what your partner may say.

Another confusing and common manipulation tactic around boundary setting is being placated by your partner (or anyone else)—in other words, when you set limits but nothing changes. They will say they are sorry, maybe make big promises to change. They may change for a short amount of time but then revert back to acting in the same hurtful ways. A pattern of disrespecting, mocking, and repeatedly violating your clear needs or limits is abusive.

If you are experiencing abuse, please know it is never your fault. The choice to be abusive is completely the other person's responsibility. It reveals the state of their capabilities, skills, and limitations rather than being a reflection of your worth. You have the right to be safe and respected at all times in all relationships—this is the purpose of your boundary-setting journey.

Aiming for a Healthy, Interdependent Relationship

True, healthy intimacy exists in an interdependent relationship—one that's balanced in your love for others with your self-care. However, you must prioritize your own self-protection because you're the only person who can tell others what hurts you or offends you. The same is true for your partner—they are the only person who can tell you what they need or want.

One of the most common boundary issues around reality in intimate relationships is the false assumption you can read others' minds to anticipate what will keep them happy—or that others are capable of and responsible for anticipating your needs without you communicating them. In a healthy relationship, each partner takes accountability to openly communicate in a respectful, clear manner.

Also, in a healthy relationship, the person who is honest about what hurts or isn't working is listened to. The person's feelings, needs, and limits are respected—even if the other person or people have a different perspective. Then a healthy compromise is sought out.

Identify Your Nonnegotiable Needs in a Relationship

Everyone has a few nonnegotiable needs in close relationships that make them feel connected and safe. Without these needs being met, you will find yourself constantly dissatisfied. Some people attempt to bypass these needs by trying to change the other person or by minimizing, judging, or ignoring their own needs. This won't work. To feel truly secure, you must honor your nonnegotiable needs. This activity will help you identify these needs.

Tools:
Piece of paper and a writing utensil

Steps:

1 Your nonnegotiable needs are 3–6 qualities you need to feel secure. These needs are authentic and unique. Only you can know what you can't compromise on in a relationship. Release any judgment around what you "should" value and instead consider—what are the things that ended past close relationships? This is a clue to what you need, such as honesty or commitment.

2 Draw a doughnut on the page (meaning, a smaller circle inside a larger one). On the outer circle, write down 1–3 things you need in any close relationship—not necessarily a romantic one—to feel secure. You may need everyone to be trustworthy.

3 Now in the inner circle write down 1–3 things you can't compromise on in a romantic/sexual partnership in addition to the previous qualities. Perhaps you need everyone you're close with to value mental health, but only a romantic partner needs to share your religion.

4 Keep this list handy moving forward. If someone doesn't meet even one nonnegotiable need, neither of you is "right" or "wrong." Still, you must accept reality in order to be safe for you and them, and act on the knowledge that a relationship is probably not a good fit. Denying your needs is self-sabotage and trying to change someone else is a boundary violation.

Address Resentment

Couples commonly seek therapy to reduce the resentment that has festered in their relationship. While anger naturally arises when a boundary has been violated or a need unmet, resentment is something a person does to themselves by not expressing or honoring their needs or limits. Sadly, countless relationships have ended because of resentment. Yet you may effectively intervene on the toxic cycle of resentment by asserting your needs and boundaries. This activity will support you.

Steps:

1 Where is resentment taking root in your relationship? Note: It doesn't need to be a romantic partnership.
   - Thoughts like "It must be nice to be able to (relax, have fun, have time for a hobby)" and "The buck stops with me" are signs that your relationship feels inequitable to you.
   - If you are keeping score of how much you and your partner are doing, this is another sign of resentment.

2 Where do you feel like there's too much on your plate compared to your partner? Use this as a sign of what you need to assert. For example, if you feel like all the housework or after-school activities are on you, there's a need to express.

3 If there are multiple causes for resentment, pick one topic at a time. This helps you remain effective while reducing overwhelm and defensiveness in the listener.

4 You always have options. Weigh the pros and cons of asserting your need for help. Notice the importance of speaking up.

5 Visualize the relief of having a more balanced relationship that you are empowered to co-create.

6 Use the script from the Assert Your Limits exercise in Chapter 1 to assert your need. Alternatively, you may feel ready to modify the script to feel more natural. Example: "I've been taking the kids to soccer and dance, and I'm overwhelmed. I need your help. Would you be willing to take over one of these activities?" Note: If there's pushback, you can seek to find a compromise that feels right to both of you.

7 Healthy boundaries are secure yet flexible. Negotiate wherever you can while validating your partner. Yet reinforce your need. Set internal limits on any urge to placate your partner and give up your needs. Asserting your needs, and finding compromise, is a cornerstone of healthy relationships. Example: "I understand you've been working late and that's stressful, yet I've had to go to work early to be the one who is always transporting our kids. It's important to me that we are both involved in their activities and sharing the responsibilities of our family. I need you to take over one of the kids' activities."

8 When negotiating with your partner (or anyone else) after you assert yourself, it's not your job to come up with solutions for the other person on how to meet your needs. Rather, let them identify solutions and options to meet your needs.

9 Then let your partner (or relevant person) follow through with organizing how they will meet their part of the responsibilities. Example: "You are willing to take care of soccer on Tuesdays? Great! Thank you for compromising with me. I really appreciate it." If your partner violates their agreement to you, then you may initially choose to remind them. You may also clarify a consequence if this happens again if you haven't already expressed this consequence. It can be hard to think of consequences, but try to make them natural. Example: "You called me at the last minute to take the kids to soccer today even though you agreed to take care of soccer on Tuesdays. I need you to respect my time at work, just as I'm respecting yours on the other days. If you don't follow through on this agreement again, I won't be available the next day to take care of the multiple activities that day. It will be your responsibility."

You Deserve to Be Heard

Validate any anxiety you may have about "rocking the boat," i.e., upsetting or burdening your partner. Remind yourself that you have the right to express your needs and have an equitable relationship. Your needs are as important as theirs—you shouldn't have to bend over backward and change your needs to be accepted.

Accept Support

Healthy relationships are interdependent, which means each person's sense of giving and receiving are balanced. Each person feels mutually supported and senses their partner puts in an equitable amount of effort into their life together. People with porous boundaries frequently feel discomfort or guilt about receiving help, which is a barrier to interdependency. Learning to receive support is a skill you can strengthen, and this activity will help you work on it. Keep practicing receiving—it's essential for all kinds of healthy relationships.

Tools:
Mirror

Steps:

1 Do you ever feel uncomfortable receiving others' attention, time, or energy? Validate if you ever feel more comfortable being the one who is giving (either literally or emotionally) in a relationship, such as by being the shoulder to cry on.

2 To be prepared for the next time someone offers to help you and it's authentically useful, practice simply saying, "That would be great; thank you!" in front of a mirror. You could also visualize letting this loving supportive energy into your heart if you'd like.

3 If you ever find yourself having an urge to reject an offer of help or micromanage how that person gives you help on a simple task, distract yourself or self-soothe. Affirm your right to receive and others' right to do things in their own way (e.g., load the dishwasher differently).

Respond to Disregarded Boundaries

Even after you learn to set boundaries, your work is not done. Every once in a while, you'll find that someone makes a mistake or completely disregards your needs or limits. When these issues arise, it can be very confusing and overwhelming. To assist you, this activity will help you identify how to best respond if your limits are disregarded after you have asserted them.

Steps:

1 As a first step for a "first offense," try taking a light approach. After all, even safe people make mistakes, so try not to assume the very worst. Remind the person of your boundary. You could say something like:
   - "Mom, you were doing so well not asking questions about my dating life, but it looks like your curiosity got the best of you. No problem, but please remember I don't want to talk about my dating life unless I bring it up."
   - "You agreed to take the kids to soccer on Tuesdays, but you called me at the last minute to do it instead. I need you to follow through on helping with the kids as you promised."

2 If someone guilt-trips you, validate yourself. Reset the boundary firmly:
   - "My need for privacy isn't about my love for you, Mom. I really hope you'll respect my need moving forward."
   - "I understand that you're busy at work, but I have a lot of responsibilities too. Our kids are one of our mutual responsibilities. It's important you help with their activities."

3 If the boundary keeps being violated, resist the urge to keep reminding them. This is not your job and you hurt your own self-respect if you beg others to respect you. Instead, enforce the consequence by saying something like:
   - "Mom, I let you know I don't want to talk about my dating life. I'm going to end the call now and I'll talk to you later."
   - "You said you can't help on Tuesdays after all with soccer. This means that I'm going to be further behind in my own work. I'm going to leave on Saturday afternoons to work in a coffee shop and you'll be on kid duty."

4 If someone continues to disregard your limit despite the consequence, follow up with more information on how you feel. It's natural to have the urge to sweep the issue under the rug, but this will hurt your relationship. Share how their choices are impacting the relationship, and what further consequences might be necessary. Here are some examples:

- "You keep asking personal questions when I asked you not to. This makes it seem like your curiosity is more important than my sense of feeling respected. This makes me not want to talk to you as often."
- "When you don't help with the kids, it sends me the message that you think I'm the one responsible for the daily care of our kids. This lack of respect makes me think we need couples therapy."

5 If all else fails, work to accept reality. You can't force someone to respect your boundaries, but you can manage the consequences of their decision. Explore your options and do what's best for your health and well-being.

Determine If Your Partner Is Behaving Safely

When you set a boundary, you always discover how safe or unsafe the relationship is for you. Learning how to notice the signs of safety, or the lack thereof, and responding accordingly is essential in order to balance self-protection alongside the protection of your intimate relationships. However, it's natural to feel confused or uncertain at times about whether this relationship is truly safe or unsafe for you. In this activity, you will gain the tools to assess the safety of your relationships to minimize confusion or self-doubt.

Tools:
Piece of paper and a writing utensil

Steps:

1 On your piece of paper, draw a line down the middle to make two columns. Label the top of the left column Signs of Safety. Label the right side Signs of a Lack of Safety. In this exercise, you will go through the various questions and mark which side your partner's behaviors belong on, whether it's the safe or unsafe category. All people make mistakes, but we are looking for a pattern in your partner's behaviors.

2 **Safe people take genuine accountability.** This means that even if they initially struggle with defensiveness, they'll take a break until they are able to truly apologize and validate your needs. They will actively work to stop behaviors that hurt you, e.g., they attend anger management classes. All people are imperfect and safe people will make mistakes. However, they will acknowledge this and keep working to meet your needs. Is your partner taking genuine accountability? If so, please note this in the Signs of Safety column. If they are just giving an apology as lip service, please note this in the Signs of a Lack of Safety column.

3 **Safe people are dependable and consistent.** They don't give mixed signals. Do you ever find yourself making excuses for your partner? If so, this is a sign of a lack of safety, please note this. Otherwise, if your partner is dependable, please note this as a sign of safety.

4 **Unsafe people will often turn the issue back on you and blame you for problems.** This is a sign of gaslighting. Do you ever feel like you're the only problem in your relationship? If so, please note this as a sign of a lack of safety. Also, please have compassion for yourself if you feel like you're the problem most of the time. If you were the family Scapegoat (see the Identify Your Family Role exercise in Chapter 8) you may be more susceptible to this form of gaslighting. In this role, it's easy to make up that it's your voice, your needs, or your boundaries that are the problem rather than another person's behaviors.

5 **Safe people meet your core nonnegotiable needs.** When you picture your future self, is how your partner (or anyone else) treats you aligned with this life? If someone doesn't meet even one of your nonnegotiable needs, notice they aren't safe or aligned with your authentic best life.

6 Review your list and use your intuition. Is your partner safe or unsafe for you? In therapy, clients often spend months, even years, trying to "analyze" if their partner is safe for them. Yet if you listen to yourself the answer will be clear to you even if it's painful or inconvenient. If you notice someone isn't safe you have options:

- Leave with the knowledge that this isn't a healthy relationship for you.
- Stay, but minimize wasting precious time and emotional energy trying to change or figure out your partner. This helps create a sense of distance, which may feel safer. For instance, don't share your emotions with a partner who continues to mock them.
- Stay, but deny reality and spend countless resources—time, energy, emotions, even money—trying to "change" your partner, which you don't have the right to do.

7 Try not to deny reality or gaslight yourself. You don't have to be ready or willing to end the relationship, but you also don't need to keep questioning your reality. If you feel unsafe this is valid.

Practice Self-Care to Protect Your Relationship

Interdependency requires you to give yourself some attention, especially if there's a part of you waiting for someone else to give you a break. Furthermore, cultivating a daily self-care practice protects your relationships. You can't pour from an empty cup—this activity will help you keep your cup full to reduce resentment while being truly present for your loved ones.

Tools:
Two cups, mugs, or jars
Scrap paper or a tiny notebook
Writing utensil

Steps:

1 Is there a part of you that sometimes feels guilty about doing nice things for yourself even though you readily do them for others? If so, please validate that it's understandable why you may give your attention, time, energy, and resources to others for love, approval, or out of habit.

2 Brainstorm all the big or small ways you would love to fill your cup up, and write them on the small scraps of paper. These may include taking time to knit, read, hike, drink water, go out to lunch, stretch, or go to the movies. Whatever feels restorative, write each activity on a separate piece of scrap paper or a tiny piece of paper.

3 Now, fold up each activity to hide your writing. Place all these separate pieces of paper inside of one of your literal cups, mugs, or jars. On the outside of this container, write *Ways to fill my cup* or something else that highlights your need to be restored. On your other container, write *Ways I restored myself* or any other phrase that you prefer.

4 If you have time now, treat yourself by pulling your first activity from the cup of activities. Go enjoy yourself! Once this activity is completed, place this piece of paper in the container of "Ways I restored myself" for a visual reminder that you are setting boundaries around your time to care for your relationships! If you pull an activity that requires more time than you can truly spare right now, schedule a date for yourself to do this activity over the next week or two.

Take a Break During Arguments

Disagreements are a natural part of close relationships, since you're authentically separate human beings. Therefore, it's essential to learn how to argue effectively. Your fight-flight-freeze response is triggered when you argue with someone close to you. When that happens, the more rational part of your brain shuts off. That's why so few arguments are productive in the moment. Taking a break and revisiting the situation later is often the best option. In this activity, you'll learn an important couples therapy skill to protect your relationship during arguments.

Steps:

1 When you argue with your partner, do you ever feel compelled to solve the issue in that moment? Does it frustrate you if your partner shuts down? Alternatively, you may be the one who shuts down when you feel pushed to communicate.

2 What's the usual outcome of your arguments with your partner? Maybe you've said things you regret or have been told something hurtful.

3 Communicate with your partner about the benefits of taking breaks during an argument to protect your relationship. Point to previous ineffective arguments and say you'd like to improve the situations by taking a short break.

4 Identify together what each of you will say to designate when you need this time, e.g., "I need a break." Remember that each of you will only call the break for yourself—not your partner. (Here's a tip: If you think your partner needs a break, you probably do too.) Establish in advance how long you will take this break (e.g., 10–20 minutes), where you will go in the house to each take space, as well as where in the house you will return after this time apart. It's important to not leave the house so neither person feels abandoned.

5 When you feel overwhelmed during an argument, say the agreed-upon words, and take a break. During this break, practice self-soothing skills like deep breathing. Set limits on repeated thoughts about why your perspective is correct and your partner's is wrong. These types of thoughts would only further communication breakdowns and issues in

the relationship. Instead, take a moment to consider why your partner may be attached to their perspective. Even though you disagree, why does it make sense they think or feel that way? Having empathy and validating your partner when you return to the discussion can help you resolve the issue much more quickly.

6 After the designated time for this break, e.g., fifteen minutes, meet again in the agreed-upon spot. Try to have the conversation again using your assertive communication and listening skills, while trying to validate your partner. Work to find common ground. If you need another break, take it. This protects the relationship and is much more important than trying to solve the issue immediately.

Build Empathy

People with porous boundaries often focus on caring for others. Yet during times of conflict, it's natural to fixate on yourself and being understood—at any cost. In this activity, you will set limits on your urge to be understood so that you can be safe for your partner too.

Steps:

1 Next time there's conflict with your partner, ask yourself, *What is my partner's perspective? Why is this important to them?* Really dig deep for loving answers but try to stay objective. Example: You might think, *My spouse doesn't want me to drink because I've been mean when I'm drunk.*

2 Ask yourself if you have violated their boundaries. Example: You might realize that it's not okay to be mean even if you're drunk.

3 Practice balancing your needs alongside a desire to protect the relationship with empathy. For example, you could think, *I want to relax, and drinking helps…but I need to be kind to my partner.*

4 When you discuss the issue again, validate whatever is possible from your partner's perspective. Don't validate unacceptable behavior, however. You can balance these needs by saying something like, "I completely understand why you're nervous about my drinking since I've been mean in the past. I'm really sad I've hurt you when I'm drunk. But drinking helps me relax and I'm stressed a lot."

5 Work to find a solution that works for both of you. For example, you could say, "I can limit my drinks to a few beers a night. This way it can take the edge off after work yet I'm not too drunk to be unable to control myself."

Empathy Strengthens Relationships

Without empathy, relationships break down. Your partner may leave out of exhaustion and despair if you refuse to set limits on your urge to be understood while refusing to give them your understanding. It's important not to get stuck in all-or-nothing thinking about who is "right," as you are a team.

Set Boundaries on Sexual Pressure

Being sexually pressured by a partner is a taboo topic. People often feel embarrassed to talk about it, because the truth that it's possible for a partner to coerce you sexually or sexually assault you is rarely discussed. Please know that if your partner pressures, guilts, or coerces you into sex, you're not alone.

Someone pressuring you to have sex is a sexual boundary violation. In this activity, you will explore how to set boundaries on sexual pressure. If you may feel triggered, please take breaks, or wait to do this activity until you feel ready.

Tools:
Highlighter

Steps:

1 Read the following list of rights. Highlight any you struggle to fully accept:
   - You have the right to your own sexual preferences and orientation.
   - You have the right to decide when, how, and with whom you want to have sex.
   - You have the right to consent and the right to revoke this consent. This is true at any time, including in a long-term relationship or marriage.
   - You have the right to negotiate around condom use, pregnancy prevention, and sexual desires to ensure you feel safe. (Someone lying about using a condom is a sexual boundary violation.)
   - You have the right to consent around sexual film or photos. (Filming or taking pictures of your sexual interaction(s) without your consent and/or sharing these images without your consent are boundary violations.)

2 Growing up or even in adulthood, did you pick up any messages around the value of your sexual desirability—for example, that having sex is the way you keep a partner? Did you learn that you're obligated to have sex in a relationship? Validate why you may question your basic sexual rights at times, and why you may have forced yourself to give consent when it wasn't authentic in the past.

3 Do you feel manipulated to have sex by your partner? If they use sex to validate their attractiveness or feel "loved," these are signs they see sex as a tool to feel confident or control you, rather than an expression of intimacy. In this case, you may need support from a couples therapist to disentangle how they interpret sex and genuine closeness.

4 Decide on the limits you need to feel safe. For example, one need may be to ensure that you use condoms to prevent disease and pregnancy. Or another need may be to refrain from sex before you resolve a fight. If your "no" isn't respected, this is a highly concerning sign of abuse. Please seek couples therapy to increase safety in the relationship. If your partner is unwilling to go to therapy, you could still greatly benefit from individual therapy.

5 Explore ways to communicate bridging your right to sexual safety alongside your partner's desires. Can you negotiate ways to have physical closeness without sex—for example, perhaps cuddling or giving each other nonsexual massages? Let your partner know that you may need these things to feel sexually safe again if there's been a history of sexual pressure.

Support Rather Than Fix

Intimacy is the act of showing up fully as your authentic self and giving your loved one the space to do the same. You each allow the other to have their full human experience, which includes feeling the wide range of emotions. This also means supporting one another rather than trying to rescue the other person. In this activity, you will practice being more loving by setting limits on taking responsibility for problems and feelings that aren't yours.

Tools:
Piece of paper and a writing utensil

Steps:

1 Are there any reasons you're worried about your partner right now? Perhaps they were recently fired.

2 Write down how you have tried to solve this problem or to make them feel better. Maybe you are trying to keep your partner's spirits up.

3 Notice that you have the right to your own emotions but that the other person's emotions are not yours. This is an important step toward differentiation rather than enmeshment. Validate your own emotions. It's natural to feel worried about your partner's job loss, for example.

4 Soothe your own emotions while remembering you can't cope for your loved one. You can soothe your own sadness by journaling, for instance, but your loved one has to make the choice to self-soothe. They also have the right to not soothe themselves—and you may need to soothe your own frustration about this. Practice accepting these uncomfortable truths.

5 Affirm that your partner is responsible for coping with their emotions and solving their problems. They have the right to figure out their own path and make mistakes. Respecting this allows you to be safe for them.

6 Set limits on your urge to rescue as needed to allow others their own process. A sign of trying to rescue another person is being preoccupied with their problems or feelings and endlessly researching solutions. If you feel like you have to be someone's parent or therapist, this is a clear sign of rescuing. Being helpful, on the other hand, is being available and present to listen to the other person. However, you may need to take breaks to ensure you are self-soothing and completing other necessary tasks in your life.

CHAPTER 10

Protecting Your Community and Friendships

Your interactions with friends and beloved community connections are extremely important. In this chapter, you'll explore the boundaries that protect your sense of community, friendships, and other relationships. The importance of showing up authentically will be the primary focus, because if you don't show up as your true self, you can't experience genuine belonging with others. The activities will show you how to set internal limits on personal behaviors that make you feel disconnected from others, such as comparing yourself and judging others.

It's a very common practice, but judging others sends you the message that you're also constantly at risk of being negatively judged yourself. Such threats to belonging naturally can lead you to focus on pleasing others rather than being who you really are. You might, for example, resist speaking up about something that's bothering you to not "upset the apple cart" or "rock the boat." Yet self-silencing further feeds a sense that your thoughts and needs aren't important. The pathway to healthy boundaries requires the practice of choosing to be authentic bit by bit, which the activities of this chapter will help you do.

Loneliness and People-Pleasing

A sense of social disconnection is one of the biggest factors in depressed feelings. This disconnection can be literal loneliness and isolation, but it can also be a more internal feeling. A person can indeed feel lonely while surrounded by people—a truly painful experience. Healthy boundaries enable you to be safe with others while being safe for them as well. This process transforms social disconnection and allows you to develop and maintain lasting bonds with others that nourish you.

The cause of most social disconnection is a very common fear that other people won't like you. That's why many people go to great lengths to hide their true self. They might turn to consumption—buying the latest clothing trends, for example—as a disheartening substitute for connection. While understandable, when you hide your true self, you don't experience the true rewards of community and social bonds. Trying to "keep up with the Joneses" is a type of people-pleasing that doesn't lead to true connection.

Unless you feel accepted by others as your authentic self, you'll continue experiencing feelings of insecurity and disconnection. When you perform and conform to be accepted by others, you will naturally wonder if the people in your life would still like you if they knew the real you. Perhaps even more painfully, you may naturally not even know who the true you is when you live for others' validation and acceptance. You might find that you lose yourself in your roles or relationships without healthy boundaries.

Trust Leads to Authentic Connection

Learning to connect, accept, and show others your authentic self is a fundamental component of healthy, meaningful bonds. When you have healthy boundaries, you can feel safe doing that. You know that even if you experience rejection or betrayal, you'll survive, because you can trust your ability to self-soothe and cope. Boundaries also help you feel empowered to protect yourself by assessing people's trustworthiness over time. Trust is, most basically, the concept of believing another person has your best interest in mind and that you can rely on them. You only know if someone is trustworthy by experiencing different events, disclosing personal information in bits, and over time. For example, if you discover that someone keeps your private information private, that's a sign of trustworthiness.

Assessing trustworthiness allows you to realize that while you may have had wounding experiences that either made you overeager to connect with people or highly suspicious of others, you can find a better balance. You can avoid oversharing with those who haven't yet proven reliable, in order to prevent a porous boundary. At the same time, you can practice revealing your authentic self in stages to assess trustworthiness and prevent having walled-off boundaries. This is the practice of showing appropriate vulnerability, which is necessary to protect yourself in all your relationships.

Being (Appropriately) Vulnerable Is a Good Thing

Appropriate vulnerability enables you to set limits on giving too much to others, which often leads to resentment or one-sided relationships. All human beings need others' support and attention. Being overly independent—or dependent—is a boundary issue. Learning how to be appropriately vulnerable means that you can ask for and accept support without controlling the help you get. This type of support enables you to live with less stress and greater connection. It also strengthens your relationships, because true friends want to show up for you too.

Part of this appropriate vulnerability means that, while you should always be authentic, different people in your life may naturally see different parts of your true self. For example, you may always be genuine, yet your coworkers will see different parts of your personality than your partner or best friend. Furthermore, for safety, it's best to take a long time assessing the trustworthiness of colleagues, because the workplace is a common place for betrayal.

Alongside this appropriate vulnerability, you have the right to privacy. At times, people with porous boundaries fear that privacy is the same as secrecy. However, in all healthy relationships, there are things you will never know about the other person because they have the right to their own private thoughts and feelings. This privacy leads to healthy differentiation, rather than enmeshment.

Avoiding Perfection

Healthy boundaries require you to set limits on the idea that you can or should be perfect in your life—in your job, in your roles, in your appearances, your intellect, etc. Likewise, you can't expect to perfectly please others by always anticipating their needs, desires, or expectations. Inevitably, others will be frustrated or disappointed with you at times because you cannot accurately predict their needs—they must communicate with you. Plus, you will find that you constantly feel anxious, exhausted, and often depressed from this impossible task. Healthy boundaries provide you with the clarity that trying to please others is a never-ending—and losing—battle.

Having healthy boundaries in relationships can be very difficult especially if you carry shame for your unique, authentic self. Difficult experiences growing up (or in adulthood) that made you feel not "good enough" can understandably make you think that your authentic self is not acceptable. These wounds may have occurred in your family, as these relationships influence your sense of being acceptable in all other relationships. Or these wounds could have occurred in peer relationships, such as by being bullied, moving a lot so you didn't form close friendships, or always feeling different from your classmates.

You can find people who will accept you for your authentic self. But to experience this true belonging, you must take steps to show your real self. When you notice ways you are performing for others, or trying to be perfect, it's important to set limits on this behavior. You must stay connected to your true values and remember that you were born to experience the richness of life. This enables you to experience true belonging with others, which is the basis of the most rewarding relationships in this world.

Stop People-Pleasing

The path to living with genuine joy, peace, and satisfaction is aligning with your authentic self. You cannot live authentically—and find this true happiness—by prioritizing pleasing others over yourself. In this activity, you will find ideas on how to avoid people-pleasing and live more authentically.

Steps:

1 Do you ever feel guilty or embarrassed when you have different opinions than others? Validate why you may fear rejection—how does this make sense given your life experiences?

2 While it makes sense that you may sometimes stay silent, has your people-pleasing ever hurt your mental health or relationships? Has your silence ever impacted your physical health—for example, eating food that makes you feel sick so you don't upset a host?

3 Set limits on people-pleasing in baby steps. Practice being more authentic in social situations with the following steps:
   - **Say no gently.** You can, for example, let someone know that you prefer not to discuss a topic any further as it's stressful, or you can decline a social invitation with kind clarity (rather than resenting the person if you do go or canceling at the last moment). You can do this simply by saying something like "I won't be able to make it to the party, but thank you for inviting me."
   - **Share your honest opinions.** Start with neutral topics, such as a different perspective on a TV show or movie. You could also practice this skill by joining a group like a book club where you don't know anyone.

Reflect On Your Own Behavior

Research shows that social disconnection triggers the brain's "alarm system," which assesses threats to safety and sets off the fight-flight-freeze response. This sense of danger can be triggered by others' criticisms or rejection. Other times, a sense of belonging is threatened by personal behaviors, such as comparing yourself to others or isolating. In this exercise, you will set limits on any of your own behaviors that make you feel disconnected from others.

Tools:
Piece of paper and a writing utensil

Steps:

1 Divide your paper into three columns. Label the first column Behaviors, the second Feelings, and the third Action Steps.

2 Do you ever compare yourself to others, either positively or negatively? Write down the ways you do this in the first column.

3 In the second column, describe how these comparisons to others make you feel. Do you feel more or less connected to others when you compare yourself? It's completely natural to compare yourself to others, but you might find that this thinking habit makes you feel ashamed and thereby disconnected from others.

4 Do you ever read gossip? Or engage in gossiping with others? How so? Add these thoughts to what you already wrote in the first column.

5 In the second column of the paper, write how gossip makes you feel in your relationships. Sometimes gossip and the judgments of others that come with it send you the message (either consciously or subconsciously) that others are judging you negatively too.

6 Do any accounts on social media make you feel like who you naturally are isn't good enough? Note anything that comes up for you around social media in the first two columns as relevant.

7 Looking at your answers in the first and second columns, are there any behaviors you want to limit or any accounts you want to unfollow? Write your ideas in the third column. If you feel safe, for instance, you may talk to your best friend about how you want to gossip less.

Assess Whether Social Media
Makes You More or Less Lonely

Sadly, there is a loneliness epidemic in the United States. As of 2021, more than half of American adults (58 percent) report feeling lonely. This social isolation literally hurts: Research shows the brain processes physical pain and social disconnection in the same region. Furthermore, social isolation can negatively impact your health—its effects can be as devastating as smoking fifteen cigarettes a day! It's natural to feel embarrassed about feeling lonely, but know you're not alone. Many people feel this way. And there's nothing wrong with you—it's genuinely more difficult to make friends as an adult.

Many people use social media to stay connected with others. Ironically, research shows the more you use social media, the more socially isolated you're likely to feel! This activity will help you identify whether social media helps your loneliness or makes it worse.

Tools:
Piece of paper and a writing utensil

Steps:

1 Think about the social media apps that you use. Do you feel better/happier or worse/lonelier/sad after scrolling through them? Maybe seeing others do fun things with friends makes you feel bad for not hanging out with friends more often, for example.

2 List the pros and cons of using social media.

3 Review your list of negatives. What boundaries might you set to alleviate these concerns? Could you unfollow anyone or mute their posts? For example, you could delete your apps and only use social media on your laptop. Honor what limits you're ready to set.

4 Practice radically accepting that loneliness is a natural part of life. All people experience this emotion at times.

Recognize Inauthentic Purchases or Changes to Your Appearance

There is no shame in wanting to be accepted by others. However, when you have porous boundaries, you may understandably want to buy things to fit in with others, or change how you look to match the crowd. Unfortunately, hiding your true self prevents you from experiencing the joy, connection, and safety of true belonging. To build awareness about where you may be missing out on authentic connection, you will explore any ways your purchases or appearance might not be aligned with your true self.

Tools:
Piece of paper and a writing utensil

Steps:

1 First, let's think about material items. Are there any items you purchase to perhaps keep up with the Joneses (or the Kardashians)? This could be things like designer clothes or purses, water bottles, makeup promoted by influencers, new tech, or anything else you wouldn't buy unless you felt like you "should" to fit in. If so, write these down.

2 Did these purchases provide you acceptance with any people or groups? If so, what did that feel like? How long did this purchase "buy" you the feeling of fitting in?

3 Did you later regret any of these purchases? Estimate the cost of these performative purchases while trying to refrain from judgment. Write this on your paper.

4 Now let's switch to your appearance. Write down anything you do to your body to fit in. This includes dyeing your hair, skincare routines, gym memberships, getting fake nails, dieting, cosmetic injections, or surgery. Remember, if any of these cosmetic changes bring true joy (e.g., you love having different hair colors), this is an act of genuine authenticity and should not be noted here. Only note what you do because you feel you "should" look a certain way.

5 How do these efforts to control your body or appearance make you feel physically? How do they make you feel emotionally?

6 Write down the financial costs of these efforts to physically fit in.

7 Add the costs of your purchases to any money you spent on your appearance. Just notice this number.

8 Validate all the types of pressure you experience to be different than who you really are for others' acceptance. These may come from your family, social media, or competitive friends, for example.

Ask Before You Post

If you use social media, practice mindfulness when you post. Ask yourself, *Do I want to share? Or am I showing off or trying to prove I'm doing well (e.g., that I'm a good parent)?* If you want to post for approval, set limits. Your life matters without others' validation.

Accept Yourself As You Are Now

When you pretend to be someone you are not in order to be accepted by others, you may ultimately feel less confident. Your relationship with yourself suffers, due to feelings of self-doubt, anxiety, and depression. In this visualization, you will validate the understandable reasons you long for approval, so that you can increase your self-compassion while gaining insight into what truly matters to you. This allows you to live more authentically in all your relationships.

Steps:

1 Sit in a comfortable place and position. Take a few deep breaths and relax.

2 Imagine that you are able to move forward in time to meet yourself in your old age. Your older self has lived a full life and has learned many lessons. They have incredible wisdom about your current experiences. Prepare to listen to their insights with an open mind and heart.

3 Greet them and hear them validate you like a loving parent—they know exactly why you sometimes hide your true self.

4 Ask what they wish they would've known about the people you work so hard to be accepted by.

5 Ask what they have learned about your genuine worth.

6 Now ask what they wish they would've known about your appearance as you are now.

7 As they reach the end of their life, how do they wish they would've spent their hard-earned money instead of spending it on fitting in? Notice they validate your values.

8 Ask any other questions you may have.

9 Thank them and visualize coming back to the current moment with this future wisdom. Write down these insights if you'd like.

Set Limits on Comparisons

If you ever think you or your life isn't as good as other people's, know that it's human nature to have such thoughts. Negatively comparing yourself to others hurts your sense of community and mental health, however. This exercise will help you reflect on when you make comparisons and how to set limits on that habit.

Steps:

1 What triggers the negative comparisons you make? Maybe it's social media (even if you logically know people control what you see). Or perhaps it's certain environments, like the gym. These are just a couple examples—what's true for you?

2 How does comparing yourself to others make you feel? Many people report that it makes them feel insecure or lonely.

3 Work to set limits on comparing yourself negatively by:
- Reminding yourself all human beings are imperfect—we all have insecurities, faults, and the longing for more in one or more areas of life.
- Reframing any jealousy triggered by comparisons as an inspiring clue to your values or desires. What does your jealousy reveal you want? What steps could you take to live into your dreams based on this insight? If you're jealous of people with money, this reveals you want more financial resources. You could try to get a better-paying job, go back to school, or learn about investment, for example.

Be Discerning, Not Judgmental

When a person has porous boundaries, they often not only feel pressured to be liked by everyone—they also often want to like everyone else. Yet this isn't authentic. Some people will trigger or overwhelm them. When you accept the truth that you can neither be liked by everyone nor enjoy everyone else entirely, you notice your options for healthy self-protection. In this activity, you will explore setting limits on all-or-nothing thinking by exploring the difference between judgment and healthy discernment.

Steps:

1 Is there anyone in your life you can't stand or tend to judge? Sit with this thought for a moment while keeping in mind that it's natural to sometimes not like certain people.

2 What don't you like about this person? Listen like a loving parent rather than judging yourself.

3 You have the right to honor what does or doesn't work for you. This is your bubble from the Visualize Your Boundaries exercise in Chapter 1 in action. Do this by reframing judgment as discernment. Here's the difference:
  - Judgment is noticing someone's qualities and believing they—or you—are wrong (or right).
  - Discernment is noticing that each of you has the right to your own views and personalities. When you discern, no one is "bad," yet you can notice with clarity that this person isn't right for you.

4 You can honor your needs without making others wrong. What boundaries do you need with this person? You may need to assert yourself or take steps to create distance in the relationship, for example.

Have Genuine Fun

The importance of having fun is often overlooked. This omission is a natural consequence of hustle culture, which teaches that work should be your top priority. It's also common to feel guilty about the human desire to have fun, especially if you feel overwhelmed with responsibilities. In this activity, you will assert your right to joy.

Tools:

Piece of paper and a writing utensil
Your paper calendar or calendar app

Steps:

1 Do you ever numb yourself when you need a break, such as by scrolling, playing online games, or drinking? Do you ever feel worse after these activities? If so, notice this with compassion.

2 Authentic fun is restorative—it makes you feel energized and renewed. When you think about such activities, what comes to mind as your favorites? Maybe it's something you'd loved doing in the past, like painting. Jot down a list of options.

3 Do any immediate thoughts arise as to why you couldn't do these activities now? Honor these thoughts as natural while also validating that only you can take the necessary steps to live into your authentic best life.

4 Take a small step toward having more fun. What are you called to do? Maybe you want to see an old friend for lunch.

5 Schedule your small step to make sure it happens. If you use a paper calendar, add your idea in Sharpie or pen, so it pushes you to pause if you try to change your mind. If you use a digital calendar and can do your idea more than once, make it an automatic recurring event so you're always reminded.

Prioritize Rest

Are you ever so busy with friends on weekends or your days off that you're exhausted by the time you go back to work? This can include being busy with your children's social activities, like for soccer tournaments, and the parents you see there. If so, do you ever feel overwhelmed because it seems like you can't get enough rest or catch up on tasks at home, like laundry?

Porous boundaries with friends and community lead to an imbalance. On one end of the spectrum is a sense of total isolation, and on the other side, a person may be too busy socially to observe the basic human need to rest in order to stay physically and mentally healthy. This exercise is for those of you who schedule too much. You will take steps toward balancing the energy you give to others and allowing yourself time to recharge.

Steps:

1 First, reflect on why you overschedule yourself. Sometimes there's a deeper reason for staying busy. Do you want to look popular or like a good parent? Perhaps you're afraid of being alone with your own thoughts? Notice what's true for you.

2 Look at your schedule now. Do any days or periods of time seem overscheduled? Think about how you would feel if you canceled some events. How does your body react to that idea? Do you feel anxious or relieved? Any reactions are okay—just notice what you feel.

3 Decide where you need to set limits to have more balance. Listen to your intuition—you likely know the answer.

4 Take baby steps toward this to give yourself more rest and space. For example, maybe you stay home one Sunday a month to regroup.

> ### Limit Exhaustion
> Author and professor Brené Brown explains it's necessary for authentic self-worth "to become intentional about cultivating sleep and play, and about letting go of exhaustion as a status symbol and productivity as self-worth." By setting these limits, you are being very courageous since it's counterculture to many societal values.

Give Generously but Authentically

Healthy relationships are interdependent—your "other-care" is balanced with self-care. To ensure you have interdependent relationships with everyone in your life, it's important to give to others only when it feels aligned with your values and priorities. Whether you're offering your time, money, expertise, or effort, this exercise will teach you to stop and ask if you're doing it authentically.

Steps:

1 Do you ever deny yourself fun or restorative activities like a trip with friends because you feel responsible for the people in your life? For instance, maybe you're concerned your partner won't eat well while you're gone, so you stay back.

- How does denying yourself impact your relationships? For example, your friendships suffer because you don't make time for them, *and* you resent your partner for not being able to eat well without you.

- Consider how inauthentic giving may not only cause resentment; it also may be disempowering your loved ones. For instance, your partner doesn't learn to cook. Or perhaps if you're always on call for a friend's relationship dramas, they won't feel motivated to break the unhealthy cycle.

2 Moving forward, when you are going to give others your time, energy, or resources, ask yourself, *Is this giving authentic?* It's okay if you make a sacrifice when it feels truly meaningful to you. This is part of the balance of healthy relationships at times. If it doesn't, though, don't offer support or help—later, you will likely feel stressed or resentful. This includes being generous by being flexible with your boundaries—don't make exceptions if you may later regret it or resent the person for it.

PART 4

Moving Forward

As you complete this book, remember that the need to set boundaries never goes away. You can't become such an expert at boundary setting that you never need to set them again. In your relationships, you will always need to keep assessing your limits as boundaries are flexible and sometimes change over time. For example, your boundaries with your partner may evolve as your children age. You will also need to set boundaries when you experience new situations, opportunities, and relationships to ensure your sense of commitment to others remains balanced with your self-protection.

Change isn't linear and different experiences or evolving relationships naturally ask you to review your boundaries or grow in new ways. Stay mindful of your options (and your anger) to continue to protect yourself and your relationships. In this part, you will be asked to take two very important steps of this boundary-setting journey—setting limits on any voice that says you may have not done "enough" yet and celebrating yourself for all your hard work!

CHAPTER 11

Protecting Your Commitment to Change and Evolve

Making a commitment to focus on boundary-setting skills is truly a life-changing experience. You find you have more time, less stress, and better relationship skills. Boundary setting is also an ongoing journey, though. Your boundaries can and necessarily will evolve as you grow, learn, and experience life. We all have times in our lives when things are quiet and steady and times when everything feels like it's in upheaval. Maintaining and updating your boundaries and your connection to yourself is one way to manage these natural ebbs and flows of life.

In this chapter, you'll focus on practicing how to adjust your boundaries as needed, such as when you're facing a big life change, and how to stay connected to yourself in difficult moments. Returning to your authentic self is always the best way to decide what to do next.

Celebrating Your Progress

As you continue to work on boundary setting, you'll naturally come to points where you begin to see success. For example, maybe you have:

- Found more balance in your life because you've set boundaries around your time.
- Improved your mental and physical well-being thanks to your self-care practice.

- Learned to hear your intuition with more clarity, helping you trust yourself more.
- Felt more confident and empowered in your authentic self now.
- Developed skills to have healthier relationships with others that are more balanced, equitable, and connected.
- Learned to honor your need for safety while practicing being safe for others.
- Respected your own truths while also respecting others' reality—dialectics in action.
- Negotiated with others, as healthy boundaries are flexible.
- Discovered that misunderstandings are natural and learned to take breaks to self-soothe as needed, which protects your relationships.

Alongside these accomplishments, you might have uncovered some uncomfortable truths about some of the people in your life or potentially wounding experiences. When these feelings arise, it can be painful, complicated, and confusing. These uncomfortable feelings are actually signs you have been successful on your journey. Another such sign is noticing that some of your relationships may have gotten harder as you expressed your needs and had the opportunity to assess who is safe and unsafe for you. Finally, another profound yet painful sign of growth is encountering anger and grief over relationships with unhealthy boundaries that may have left you questioning your right to self-protection.

The Power of Forgiving Others—and Yourself

Experiencing complex feelings of grief and anger, and memories of traumatic experiences, can be very confusing. When that happens, it's important to assess how safe you are in the relationship. If you aren't safe, please continue to set boundaries, including creating distance in the relationship as you need to protect yourself.

If the person *is* safe, you may choose to contemplate forgiveness work if you're struggling to accept the past and let go of resentment. Making the choice to forgive is highly personal and you have the right to decide if it does or doesn't work for you—it's just an option worth mentioning.

Forgiveness is not saying you agree with how someone has treated you. Instead, it's radically accepting that the past happened and you can't change it—you can only prevent yourself from feeling the suffering of holding on to it. Forgiveness and boundary setting are not mutually exclusive: You can forgive someone for the past and yet still need to set boundaries with them.

If you feel stuck on past events, and the person is now safe, you could have an open, heartfelt conversation with them. But once they apologize and have genuinely changed, it's important to not keep processing this with them to be safe for them. You could instead discuss it with trusted friends or write in your journal, for example.

It's your right and decision to decide whether you want to forgive anyone else, or not. Either way, please consider forgiving *yourself*. Forgive yourself for not protecting yourself in the past. You did the best you could back then, and you made your past choices for valid reasons. Also, forgive yourself if you haven't improved as much as you think you "should" have. You can't perfectly master self-development—it's a lifelong journey.

Keep Up the Great Work!

The good news is that you cannot fail on this journey—areas where you have stumbled provide you with new information! Try reframing your "failures" as clues of your longings. For example, if you're upset with yourself because you still don't practice sustainable self-care, notice your longing for self-connection and nourishment. This gentler approach reminds you that you continue to have options.

Moving forward, please remember, you always have choices. If you feel stuck, confused, or overwhelmed about a particular boundary, return to the skills you've learned throughout this book. Stay connected to your authentic values and your nonnegotiable needs. Keep prioritizing your self-protection and asserting yourself—because you're the only one who can do this for yourself—and negotiate where you can. And keep working to listen to your intuition. Deep down, your best path will always become clear when you look within—you can trust yourself!

Review and Update Your Treasure Map

In Chapter 1, you identified goals for your boundary-setting journey in the Create Your Boundaries Treasure Map exercise. This treasure map represented a treatment plan that's often established at the beginning of therapy. Part of the healing journey involves reviewing your goals—where you started, what you've accomplished, and what you still want to achieve. Now, take a moment to review your treasure map to see your progress as well as your needs for continued growth.

Tools:

Your treasure map from the Create Your Boundaries Treasure Map exercise in Chapter 1
Writing utensil

Steps:

1 Identify your progress from your treasure map. What did you accomplish during this journey? Affirm and celebrate your hard work. Here are some examples:
   - I told my parents I couldn't visit this summer and it was a lot easier than I thought!
   - Wow, I totally forgot I hadn't been reading. I read when I take a bath a couple times a week now. This is amazing progress toward self-care!

2 Is there anything you've yet to accomplish? See this like a loving parent—self-development is always a journey of progress, not perfection. You only discover what does and doesn't work as well as where you may need extra support. What barriers have you run into? What support do you need? Add additional points to your map as needed to note this. For example:
   - My husband gets defensive when I talk about housework, and I shut down. Maybe I need to talk to him about this pattern prior to being able to effectively talk about the housework. I can create a new assertive script. I'll also check out the books on relationships in the Resources section.

3 As you review your map alongside your successes and continued needs, consider if you now have new or updated goals. If so, add them to your treasure map, along with any subgoals. If you want to make a whole new map, feel free! Part of the therapy journey is to assess your progress and to continue updating your goals as you feel called to do.

Let Your Anger Show You Your Next Boundary

Staying mindful of your anger is your best asset to reveal boundaries you may need to set in the future. Anger always highlights an unmet need or violated boundary—even if you're not yet conscious what they are. In this activity, you will discover where anger shows up in your body so you can receive the messages it's sending. As boundary setting becomes second nature thanks to your ongoing practice and focus, you can count on your anger to keep pointing to areas that need attention.

Tools:
Piece of paper and a writing utensil

Steps:

1 Draw a vague outline of a person on your piece of paper. If you have feelings of judgment that may be triggered around your body or drawing capabilities, just draw a stick figure.

2 When you're angry (frustrated, irritated, annoyed, etc.) or resentful (which is long-standing anger), practice mindfulness of your body's sensations to notice how you feel. Mark the locations you feel anger on your body outline with a star or checkmark. Physical sensations commonly associated with anger are:
   - Tightness or clenching in your jaw
   - Holding your breath
   - Seeing red
   - Your heartbeat quickening
   - Turning red
   - Squeezing your fists or upper body
   - Feeling your eyelids squeeze shut

3 When you're angry, notice these or other physical sensations; then listen to yourself like a loving parent hearing their child describe what has upset them. Validate your feelings. You might have the urge to be destructive (to yell, hit, throw things, be critical, etc.), but you don't have to act on it. Instead, self-soothe to harness the gift of anger while being safe for you and others. Denying your anger will only harm your relationships, because you will eventually explode on others or feel depressed if you keep your anger inside.

Create a Confidence Journal

One of the most powerful tools you can have as you continue to grow and change is the power of self-confidence. Self-confidence gives you self-assurance as you protect yourself, various parts of your life, and your relationships. It also empowers you to live as authentically as possible, because you believe in yourself and your choices. In this exercise, you'll create a confidence journal that you can turn to again and again to remind yourself of your innate power and worth.

Tools:

Journal or notebook
Writing utensil
Stickers or other embellishments (optional)

Steps:

1 This journal will be a home for all your wins—big or small. Here are some examples of events and feelings you can write down:

- Any time you experience proof that you are capable of being brave and assertive
- Your boundary-setting success stories
- The feelings you had when you spoke up respectfully, even though you were nervous; when, say, the restaurant got your order wrong or your contractor made a mistake
- Times you listened to your intuition, whether about your limits or other topics; this includes noticing when the path you felt called to was successful, such as after starting a podcast

2 Add decorations, pictures, or whatever else helps you record these wins!

3 Keep your confidence journal nearby so you can write in it frequently. In addition, read and review it periodically to remember all your wins and overcome self-doubt. You'll be reminded just how capable and amazing you authentically are!

Deal with Big Life Changes

Everyone faces important life changes at one point or another. Maybe you've decided to relocate to a different city, you were laid off, or you're about to welcome a new baby. Whatever the big change is—if it's going to upend your life, it'll affect your boundaries. Take a moment to stop and re-evaluate your life and needs, factoring in this event. This four-step process will help you assess what to keep and what to change as you manage the change.

Steps:

1 **Examine the boundaries you have now.** Which can stay exactly as is? For example, if you're moving in with your partner, you could maintain the boundaries you've already established on how and when you discuss difficult topics.

2 **Do any of your boundaries not apply anymore?** If so, it's okay to retire them. Your boundaries with your roommate about not eating each other's special food items can now be retired. You can thank yourself for having the courage to address this with your roommate in the past.

3 **Which boundaries need to be adjusted slightly?** For example, now that you'll be living with your partner, you will likely need to adjust how each of you can get alone time. In the past, you could just go to your separate home; now you will need to discuss that, say, when you get home from work you like a few minutes to yourself first.

4 **Which totally new boundaries do you need to add to accommodate this change?** If you're moving in with your partner, you likely will need new boundaries around shared finances. Or, if you're welcoming a new baby, you might need to set a new boundary that you leave work every day at a certain time.

Recharge Yourself When You're Drained

Since the journey of boundary setting is lifelong, you will have natural ebbs and flows in energy levels and self-confidence. In the ebbs, you may notice that you feel drained and increasingly disconnected from yourself. If that happens, notice it mindfully as soon as possible. This activity will help you reconnect with yourself and recharge when you feel drained.

Tools:

Piece of paper and markers, crayons, or colored pencils

Steps:

1 Draw a circle on your piece of paper and divide it into eight parts— this should look like a cut pie. Label each section of your pie with the following labels: My Inner Child, My Physical Health, My Mental Health, My Relationships, My Family, My Work, My Money, and My Time.

2 For each section, reflect on what you have discovered that nourishes you. You can write words in each section and/or draw pictures. Have fun with celebrating your increased self-awareness. For example, if you have discovered that your inner child needs time to just be, you could write words like "Space" or "Freedom." Maybe you draw a picture of yourself watching clouds to represent this need as well. Or for My Mental Health you may now know that you need to ensure you get enough sleep. Of course, this may overlap with your physical health as well. That's okay— sometimes the same activity nourishes different areas of your life.

3 Once you have filled in every section of your pie, take a moment to reflect on how far you've come. How different do you think this drawing may have looked when you picked this book up for the first time? You likely know so much more about who you are and what you need in life!

4 Keep this visual handy, like on your nightstand or hung up on a bulletin board. Whenever you feel depleted or burnt-out, return to this picture. Scan this drawing, knowing that the answers for restoration are right here. Take the first step that jumps out to you from this drawing to replenish yourself—it may be, for example, to clear your Sunday morning so you can sleep in. Repeat this practice as often as you need, remembering that there will be natural ebbs and flows in your relationship with yourself.

Celebrate Yourself

Boundary setting helps nourish your basic physical needs and care for your emotions—but it also allows you to have more fun and fully enjoy your life! This activity helps you specifically set boundaries around your time so you can fully celebrate yourself.

Tools:
Piece of paper and a writing utensil

Steps:

1 Brainstorm a list of all the fun things you've always wanted to do. These ideas can range from the small and inexpensive to large, extravagant ones. You needn't figure out how you will be able to do all these activities. For example, you might want to go to an art museum, take a painting class, or visit the country of your ancestry.

2 Affirm aloud that, "I have the right to enjoy my life!" You can say this in the mirror, shout it joyfully, or just say it internally. Enjoying your life is part of why you have worked hard to cultivate healthy boundaries.

3 If you have mixed feelings when you look at your list, recognize them. Set limits on the voice that is telling you why you *can't* do these things. Instead, lean into feelings of joy, hope, or excitement.

4 Pick one activity off your list and schedule it. It can be big or small— pick what you authentically want and are able to do right now. As you plan and execute this idea, continually come back to the fact that you're doing it to celebrate your boundary-setting success.

You Deserve It!
Part of you might feel silly or extravagant celebrating yourself. If so, validate this part while setting limits on it. Taking time to celebrate yourself in life is an aspect of having healthy boundaries. You deserve a celebration!

Conclusion

Congratulations! You have worked incredibly hard through the exercises in this book. Your courageous choice to push through the discomfort of learning a new skill has allowed you to strengthen your boundaries.

Hopefully, you are arriving to the end of this book with a lot of pride and appreciation for yourself. You have done tremendously difficult therapeutic work—work that many people never do—to get to this point. Wherever you find yourself now, enjoy where you are now. There is no right or wrong way to be completing this book, because change isn't linear.

Please take time to pause and celebrate your progress. Enjoy the view of whatever mountaintop your journey has led you to. You can live your life continuing to practice and integrate your new skills while climbing different mountains.

Later on, if you decide that you have more work to do, you can return to therapy or self-development work. The Resources section of this book will support you in that quest. But for now, enjoy your progress and celebrate your authentic self!

Resources

Inner Child Work and Self-Compassion

Brown, Brené. (2010). *The Gifts of Imperfection: Let Go of Who You Think You're Supposed to Be and Embrace Who You Are*. Center City, MN: Hazelden.

Brown, Brené. (2012). *Daring Greatly: How the Courage to Be Vulnerable Transforms the Way We Live, Love, Parent, and Lead*. New York: Avery.

Neff, Kristin. (2011). *Self-Compassion: The Proven Power of Being Kind to Yourself*. New York: William Morrow.

Neff, Kristin. (2021). *Fierce Self-Compassion: How Women Can Harness Kindness to Speak Up, Claim Their Power, and Thrive*. New York: Harper Wave.

Taylor, Cathryn L. (1991). *The Inner Child Workbook: What to Do with Your Past When It Just Won't Go Away*. New York: Jeremy P. Tarcher/Putnam.

Protecting Your Reality and Being More Authentic

Brown, Brené. (2010). *The Gifts of Imperfection: Let Go of Who You Think You're Supposed to Be and Embrace Who You Are*. Center City, MN: Hazelden.

Cameron, Julia. (2016). *The Artist's Way: A Spiritual Path to Higher Creativity*. New York: TarcherPerigee.

Confidently Authentic. ConfidentlyAuthentic.com.

Doyle, Glennon. (2020). *Untamed*. New York: The Dial Press.

Kahneman, Daniel. (2011). *Thinking, Fast and Slow*. New York: Farrar, Straus and Giroux.

Mazzola Wood, Krystal. (2022, November 22). "How to Spot the Hidden Signs Someone Is Gaslighting You." *Confidently Authentic.* https://confidently authentic.com/how-to-spot-the-hidden-signs-someone-is-gaslighting-you.

Molfino, Majo. (2020). *Break the Good Girl Myth: How to Dismantle Outdated Rules, Unleash Your Power, and Design a More Purposeful Life.* New York: HarperOne.

Protecting Your Time and Practicing Self-Care

Mazzola Wood, Krystal. (2022, February 28). "How to Take Care of Yourself—6 Simple Self-Care Strategies." *Confidently Authentic.* https://confidentlyauthentic.com/how-to-self-care.

Mazzola Wood, Krystal. (2022, June 27). "Why Self-Care Is Not Selfish." *Confidently Authentic.* https://confidentlyauthentic.com/why-self-care-is-not-selfish.

Rodsky, Eve. (2021). *Find Your Unicorn Space: Reclaim Your Creative Life in a Too-Busy World.* New York: G.P. Putnam's Sons.

Williams, Florence. (2017). *The Nature Fix: Why Nature Makes Us Happier, Healthier, and More Creative.* New York: W.W. Norton & Company.

Zomorodi, Manoush. (2017). *Bored and Brilliant: How Spacing Out Can Unlock Your Most Productive and Creative Self.* New York: St. Martin's Press.

Protecting Your Mental Health

Brach, Tara. (2003). *Radical Acceptance: Embracing Your Life with the Heart of a Buddha.* New York: Bantam Dell.

Cronin, Elizabeth. (2022). *Mindfulness Journal for Mental Health: Prompts and Practices to Improve Your Well-Being.* Oakland, CA: Rockridge Press.

David, Susan. (2017, November 3). *The Gift and Power of Emotional Courage* [Video]. TED Conferences. https://ted.com/talks/susan_david_the_gift_and_power_of_emotional_courage?language=en.

Hanh, Thich Nhat. (2016). *Silence: The Power of Quiet in a World Full of Noise.* New York: HarperOne.

Kabat-Zinn, Jon. (1994). *Wherever You Go, There You Are: Mindfulness Meditation in Everyday Life*. New York: Hyperion.

Khedr, Mahmoud. (2019, November 22). *How Toxic Positivity Leads to More Suffering* [Video]. TEDx Talks. https://youtube.com/watch?v=5EOj2Z7hw5w.

Mazzola Wood, Krystal. (2022, August 8). "What to Do If You Can't Afford Therapy: 4 Effective Tips from a Therapist." *Confidently Authentic*. https://confidentlyauthentic.com/what-to-do-if-you-cant-afford-therapy.

McKay, Matthew, Jeffrey C. Wood, and Jeffrey Brantley. (2007). *The Dialectical Behavior Therapy Skills Workbook: Practical DBT Exercises for Learning Mindfulness, Interpersonal Effectiveness, Emotion Regulation, and Distress Tolerance*. Oakland, CA: New Harbinger.

Tolle, Eckhart. (1997). *The Power of Now: A Guide to Spiritual Enlightenment*. Vancouver: Namaste Publishing.

Trauma Healing

The Bare Female [Free yoga videos]. https://youtube.com/@TheBareFemale.

van der Kolk, Bessel. (2014). *The Body Keeps the Score: Brain, Mind, and Body in the Healing of Trauma*. New York: Viking Penguin.

Yoga with Adriene [Free yoga videos]. https://youtube.com/user/yogawithadriene.

Protecting Your Body

Innanen, Summer. *Eat the Rules* [Podcast]. https://summerinnanen.com/etr.

Protecting Your Money and Contributions

Dunlap, Tori. (2022). *Financial Feminist: Overcome the Patriarchy's Bullsh*t to Master Your Money and Build a Life You Love*. New York: Dey Street Books.

Dunlap, Tori. *Her First $100K* [Podcast]. https://herfirst100k.com.

Sethi, Ramit. (2009). *I Will Teach You to Be Rich*. New York: Workman Publishing.

Protecting Your Relationships with Family

Mazzola, Krystal. (2019). *The Codependency Recovery Plan: A 5-Step Guide to Understand, Accept, and Break Free from the Codependent Cycle.* Emeryville, CA: Althea Press.

Mazzola, Krystal. (2020). *The Codependency Workbook: Simple Practices for Developing and Maintaining Your Independence.* Emeryville, CA: Rockridge Press.

Protecting Your Intimate Relationships and Dating Skills

Behary, Wendy T. (2021). *Disarming the Narcissist: Surviving and Thriving with the Self-Absorbed.* Oakland, CA: New Harbinger.

Levine, Amir and Rachel Heller. (2010). *Attached: The New Science of Adult Attachment and How It Can Help You Find—and Keep—Love.* New York: TarcherPerigee.

Mazzola, Krystal. (2019). *The Codependency Recovery Plan: A 5-Step Guide to Understand, Accept, and Break Free from the Codependent Cycle.* Emeryville, CA: Althea Press.

Mazzola, Krystal. (2020). *The Codependency Workbook: Simple Practices for Developing and Maintaining Your Independence.* Emeryville, CA: Rockridge Press.

Mazzola Wood, Krystal. *Confidently Authentic* [Blog]. ConfidentlyAuthentic.com.

Ruiz, don Miguel. (1997). *The Four Agreements: A Practical Guide to Personal Freedom.* San Rafael, CA: Amber-Allen.

Tallon-Hicks, Yana. (2022). *Hot and Unbothered: How to Think about, Talk about, and Have the Sex You Really Want.* New York: Harper Wave.

The Gottman Institute: A Research-Based Approach to Relationships [Workshops and blog]. https://gottman.com.

The Healthy Relationship Foundation [Workshops and blog]. https://healthyrelationshipfoundation.com.

The Love Fix [Podcast]. https://thelovefix.com/listen.

Protecting Your Community and Friendships

Dr. Marisa G. Franco [Blog on friendship and relationships]. https://drmarisagfranco.com.

Franco, Marisa G. (2022). *Platonic: How the Science of Attachment Can Help You Make—and Keep—Friends*. New York: G.P. Putnam's Sons.

Finding a Therapist

Psychology Today Directory. https://psychologytoday.com/us/therapists (can search by area, specializations, insurance, and other filters).

References

How to Use This Book:

Kahneman, Daniel. (2011). *Thinking, Fast and Slow*. New York: Farrar, Straus and Giroux.

Chapter 2:

Mazzola, Krystal. (2019). *The Codependency Recovery Plan: A 5-Step Guide to Understand, Accept, and Break Free from the Codependent Cycle*. Emeryville, CA: Althea Press.

Mazzola, Krystal. (2020). *The Codependency Workbook: Simple Practices for Developing and Maintaining Your Independence*. Emeryville, CA: Rockridge Press.

Mellody, Pia. (2003). *Facing Codependence: What It Is, Where It Comes From, How It Sabotages Our Lives*. New York: HarperSanFrancisco.

Chapter 3:

Attkisson, Sharyl. (2015, February 6). *Astroturf and Manipulation of Media Messages* [Video]. TEDx Talks. https://youtube.com/watch?v=-bYAQ-ZZtEU.

Connolly, Maureen. (2023, April 25). "ADHD in Girls: The Symptoms That Are Ignored in Females." *ADDitude Magazine*. https://additudemag.com/adhd-in-girls-women.

Mazzola, Krystal. (2020). *The Codependency Workbook: Simple Practices for Developing and Maintaining Your Independence*. Emeryville, CA: Rockridge Press.

Mazzola Wood, Krystal. (2022, November 22). "How to Spot the Hidden Signs Someone Is Gaslighting You." *Confidently Authentic.* https://confidentlyauthentic.com/how-to-spot-the-hidden-signs-someone-is-gaslighting-you.

Mellody, Pia. (2003). *Facing Codependence: What It Is, Where It Comes From, How It Sabotages Our Lives.* New York: HarperSanFrancisco.

Molfino, Majo. (2020). Chapter 6: The Myth of Logic. In *Break the Good Girl Myth: How to Dismantle Outdated Rules, Unleash Your Power, and Design a More Purposeful Life.* New York: HarperOne.

Quinn, Patricia and Sharon Wigal. (2004, May 4). "Perceptions of Girls and ADHD: Results from a National Survey." *Medscape General Medicine,* 6(2), 2. PMID: 15266229, PMCID: PMC1395774.

Witvliet, Margot Gage. (2022, October 23). "How COVID-19 Brought Medical Gaslighting to the Forefront and Made Invisible Illness Visible: Lessons from the BIPOC Long COVID Study." In S. Palermo & B. Olivier (Eds.), *COVID-19 Pandemic, Mental Health and Neuroscience—New Scenarios for Understanding and Treatment.* IntechOpen. https://doi.org/10.5772/intechopen.107936.

Chapter 4:

Hanh, Thich Nhat. (2016). *Silence: The Power of Quiet in a World Full of Noise.* New York: HarperOne.

Heshmat, Shahram. (2020, April 4). "5 Benefits of Boredom." *Psychology Today.* https://psychologytoday.com/us/blog/science-choice/202004/5-benefits-boredom.

Mark, Gloria, Daniela Gudith, and Ulrich Klocke. (2008, April). "The Cost of Interrupted Work: More Speed and Stress." In *Proceedings of the SIGCHI Conference on Human Factors in Computing Systems,* 107–110. https://doi.org/10.1145/1357054.1357072.

Pattison, Kermit. (2008, July 28). "Worker, Interrupted: The Cost of Task Switching." *Fast Company.* https://fastcompany.com/944128/worker-interrupted-cost-task-switching.

Chapter 5:

Brach, Tara. (2003). *Radical Acceptance: Embracing Your Life with the Heart of a Buddha*. New York: Bantam Dell.

Bradt, Steve. (2010, November 11). "Wandering Mind Not a Happy Mind." *The Harvard Gazette*. https://news.harvard.edu/gazette/story/2010/11/wandering-mind-not-a-happy-mind.

Hanh, Thich Nhat. (2016). *Silence: The Power of Quiet in a World Full of Noise*. New York: HarperOne.

Kabat-Zinn, Jon. (1994). *Wherever You Go, There You Are: Mindfulness Meditation in Everyday Life*. New York: Hyperion.

Mazzola, Krystal. (2019). *The Codependency Recovery Plan: A 5-Step Guide to Understand, Accept, and Break Free from the Codependent Cycle*. Emeryville, CA: Althea Press.

van der Kolk, Bessel. (2014). *The Body Keeps the Score: Brain, Mind, and Body in the Healing of Trauma*. New York: Viking Penguin.

Chapter 6:

Armstrong, Lawrence E. et al. (2012, February). "Mild Dehydration Affects Mood in Healthy Young Women." *Journal of Nutrition*, 142(2), 382–388. https://doi.org/10.3945/jn.111.142000.

Gordon, Amie M. and Serena Chen. (2013, May). "The Role of Sleep in Interpersonal Conflict: Do Sleepless Nights Mean Worse Fights?" *Social Psychological and Personality Science*, 5(2), 168–175. https://doi.org/10.1177/1948550613488952.

Mazzola Wood, Krystal. (2022, February 28). "How to Take Care of Yourself—6 Simple Self-Care Strategies." *Confidently Authentic*. https://confidentlyauthentic.com/how-to-self-care.

Mazzola Wood, Krystal. (2022, June 27). "Why Self-Care Is Not Selfish." *Confidently Authentic*. https://confidentlyauthentic.com/why-self-care-is-not-selfish.

Chapter 7:

Achor, Shawn and Michelle Gielan. (2016, July 13). "The Data-Driven Case for Vacation." *Harvard Business Review*. https://hbr.org/2016/07/the-data-driven-case-for-vacation.

Alhola, Paula and Päivi Polo-Kantola. (2007, October). "Sleep Deprivation: Impact on Cognitive Performance." *Neuropsychiatric Disease and Treatment*, 3(5), 553–567. PMID: 19300585, PMCID: PMC2656292.

Cooper, Christopher B. et al. (2018, October 4). "Sleep Deprivation and Obesity in Adults: A Brief Narrative Review." *BMJ Open Sport & Exercise Medicine*, 4(1), e000392. https://doi.org/10.1136/bmjsem-2018-000392.

Dong, Lu, Yongwei Xie, and Xiaohua Zou. (2022, January 1). "Association Between Sleep Duration and Depression in US Adults: A Cross-Sectional Study." *Journal of Affective Disorders*, 296. 183–188. https://doi.org/10.1016/j.jad.2021.09.075.

Gordon, Amie M. and Serena Chen. (2013, May). "The Role of Sleep in Interpersonal Conflict: Do Sleepless Nights Mean Worse Fights?" *Social Psychological and Personality Science*, 5(2), 168–175. https://doi.org/10.1177/1948550613488952.

Grandner, Michael A. et al. (2016, September). "Sleep: Important Considerations for the Prevention of Cardiovascular Disease." *Current Opinion in Cardiology*, 31(5), 551–565. https://doi.org/10.1097/HCO.0000000000000324.

Kahneman, Daniel. (2011). *Thinking, Fast and Slow*. New York: Farrar, Straus and Giroux.

Kochhar, Rakesh, Kim Parker, and Ruth Igielnik. (2022, July 28). "Majority of US Workers Changing Jobs Are Seeing Real Wage Gains." *Pew Research Center*. https://pewresearch.org/social-trends/2022/07/28/Majority-of-u-s-workers-changing-jobs-are-seeing-real-wage-gains.

Mazzola, Krystal. (2019). *The Codependency Recovery Plan: A 5-Step Guide to Understand, Accept, and Break Free from the Codependent Cycle*. Emeryville, CA: Althea Press.

Chapter 9:

Levine, Amir and Rachel Heller. (2010). *Attached: The New Science of Adult Attachment and How It Can Help You Find—and Keep—Love.* New York: TarcherPerigee.

Chapter 10:

Brown, Brené. (2010). *The Gifts of Imperfection: Let Go of Who You Think You're Supposed to Be and Embrace Who You Are.* Center City, MN: Hazelden.

Eisenberger, Naomi I. and Steve W. Cole. (2012, April 15). "Social Neuroscience and Health: Neurophysiological Mechanisms Linking Social Ties with Physical Health." *Nature Neuroscience,* 15, 669–674. https://doi.org/10.1038/nn.3086.

Franco, Marisa G. (2020, February 16). "5 Skills for Making Friends As an Adult." *Dr. Marisa G. Franco.* https://drmarisagfranco.com/5-skills-for-making-friends-as-an-adult.

Holt-Lunstad, Julianne. (2021, May 4). *Is Social Disconnection Comparable to Smoking?* [Video]. TEDx Talks. www.ted.com/talks/julianne_holt_lunstad_is_social_disconnection_comparable_to_smoking.

Primack, Brian A. et al. (2017, March 6). "Social Media Use and Perceived Social Isolation among Young Adults in the US." *American Journal of Preventive Medicine,* 53(1), 1–8. https://doi.org/10.1016/j.amepre.2017.01.010.

The Cigna Group. (2023). *The Loneliness Epidemic Persists: A Post-Pandemic Look at the State of Loneliness among US Adults.* https://newsroom.thecignagroup.com/loneliness-epidemic-persists-post-pandemic-look.

Index